Individualized Learning
with Technology

Individualized Learning with Technology

Meeting the Needs of High School Students

2nd Edition

Christine Bernat

ROWMAN & LITTLEFIELD
Lanham • Boulder • New York • London

Published by Rowman & Littlefield
An imprint of The Rowman & Littlefield Publishing Group, Inc.
4501 Forbes Boulevard, Suite 200, Lanham, Maryland 20706
www.rowman.com

6 Tinworth Street, London SE11 5AL, United Kingdom

Copyright © 2019 by Christine Bernat

All rights reserved. No part of this book may be reproduced in any form or by any electronic or mechanical means, including information storage and retrieval systems, without written permission from the publisher, except by a reviewer who may quote passages in a review.

British Library Cataloguing in Publication Information Available

Library of Congress Cataloging-in-Publication Data Available

ISBN 978-1-4758-5193-9 (cloth)
ISBN 978-1-4758-5194-6 (pbk.)
ISBN 978-1-4758-5195-3 (electronic)

Contents

Preface ix

Acknowledgments xi

1   Needed: A Revolution in Learning   1
    Technology Allows for Control   2
    From Pedagogy to Andragogy   3
    The Need for Lifelong Learning   4
    More Technology for Adolescents and Adults   6

2   Using All of the Mind   9
    Improving Semantic Memory   9
    Improving Episodic Memory   11
    Improving Procedural Memory   12
    What Is Intelligence?   14
        From Fluid to Crystallized Intelligence   15
        The Multifactor or Aptitudes   16
        Realizing Adaptation and "Street-Smarts"   17

3   Enhancing Knowledge Development   20
    Better Conceptual Learning   20
    Better Organization of Knowledge   22
    Meeting Learner Characteristics   23
        Readiness to Learn   24
        Cultural Background   24
        Learner Rate and Style   25
    Standards Are Limiting   26

4	Providing for Experience—It's the Best Teacher	30
	Better Learning through the Senses	30
	Going from Pictures to Words to Pictures Again	31
	Using Media to Enhance Learning	32
	Sesame Street—Media in Learning	33
	Creating a Knowledge Base	34
	Learning through Modeling	35
	Experiencing Positive Cases	36
	Learning in the Affective Domain	37
5	Improving Basic Skills	41
	The Rise of Programmed Instruction	41
	Teaching Is an Art and a Science	42
	Improving Academic Skills	43
	Improving Real-World Skills	43
	Learning Must Be "Rewarding"	45
	More Intrinsic Rewarding	45
	Going from Extrinsic to Intrinsic Rewards	48
	The Control Must Be with the Learner	49
6	Improving Higher-Order Skills	52
	Improving Deductive Reasoning	52
	Practicing with Algorithms	54
	Improving Inductive Reasoning	54
	Practicing with Heuristics	55
	Improving Reflective Reasoning	56
	Improving Critical Thinking in All Areas	58
	Feeling the Rewards of Critical Thinking	59
	More Targeted Learning for Adults	61
7	Enhancing Attention and Perception	65
	Improving Perception	65
	Improving How Information Is Processed	67
	Improving How Information Is Stored	68
	Improving How Information Is Managed	69
	Improving Meta-Cognition and Motivation	70
	Better Meta-Cognition for Better Learning	71
	Improving Study Skills	71
	Promoting Self-Directed Learning	72
	Enhancing Motivation—The Real Maker of Achievement	73
	Promote Mastery to Improve Motivation	73
	Promote Purpose to Improve Motivation	74

8	Promoting Better Memory and Assessment	77
	Make Learning Distinctive	78
	Make Information Meaningful	78
	Use Mnemonics and Stories to Improve Memory	80
	Preventing Forgetting	81
	Put Learning into Context	82
	Improving Testing	83
	Utilize Performance Methods	84
9	Applications for Skill-Building	88
	Drill-and-Practice	88
	Simulations	89
	Games	91
	Reflective "Buggy" Models	93
	Artificial Intelligence	94
	Computers and People Working Together	96
10	Applications for Individualizing Instruction	99
	Tutoring Is Individualized Learning	99
	Less Structured vs. More Structured Approaches	100
	Empowering Environments	101
	Internet Learning	102
	Distance Learning	104
	Computer-Assisted Instruction (CAI)	105
	Blended Learning	106
	More Individualized Learning in the Future	107
11	Conclusion	110
	Improving Knowledge-based Learning	111
	Improving Experiential-based Learning	113
	Improving Skill-Based Learning	114
	Promoting Self-Directed and Lifelong Learning	115
Index		117
About the Authors		121

Preface

This book is the result of a collaborative effort between my father's writing and my own. After my father, Richard J. Mueller, retired from a thirty-year career as a professor of educational psychology in the mid-1990s, he decided to write a textbook. His textbook would contain all of the typical educational psychology material, but he wanted to add additional information about two powerful trends emerging within the field of education. Those trends were the increasing use of technology for teaching and learning, and the rise of the adult learner, who would require continuous learning throughout life.

Together, these two monumental trends would exert enormous pressure on change to the standard ways of teaching and learning. Specifically, they would push learning beyond the three Rs, they would demand alternatives to the pedagogies of classroom instruction, and they would require new assessments beyond the group-ranking of standardized testing.

My father finished his textbook, but it was never published. Not long after that time, he developed cancer and died. But I, his daughter, took an interest in his book. I had been working as an instructional designer and technical writer for over ten years. I was witnessing the real-world results of the trends my father had researched and written about in his book. Within business and industry, computers were being used more frequently as a tool for specialized training, and workers were increasingly needing continuous learning to "keep up" throughout their lives.

That is the reason that I decided to write this book. I wanted to use much of my father's research and background in education, along with my insights on the future of adult learning and professional development. Together, I believe this book has a good mix of the theoretical and practical that can be of benefit to any educator. It can be a meaningful start for educators involved in public education at the secondary level to move into better meeting the learning needs of the twenty-first century.

In this second edition of this book, I have condensed much of what was in the first edition. I have been careful to retain only the information that I believe can be most useful to educators. I have eliminated much of the background information about the information revolution and to the changes that have resulted from it to our modern world. Everyone is well aware of what the information revolution is all about. The question now becomes, how can we meet the needs of the twenty-first-century learner, especially when there is such a diverse population of students within the United States, and with ever limited budgets?

Education reform can't happen immediately. That is why this book focuses only on making change at the high school level, and with most of the change happening in the final two years of high school. If the focus of change is directed at the secondary level, then much of what has been contained in traditional education and which has been successful for hundreds of years can remain the same. It is a way of staying the course while also making the necessary changes to meet the needs of the twenty-first-century learner. I hope that you find this book useful and helpful.

Acknowledgments

I want to thank my family for their encouragement during the writing of this book. My husband Tom, son Neil, and daughter Brooke have been very supportive. I'd especially like to thank my inquisitive son for his questions directed at specific content of the book, and to my very artistic daughter for her inspiration on the idea for the cover of the book. Lastly, I'd like to specially acknowledge my father for his tireless efforts to research ways to improve education. A phrase he was fond of saying as I was growing up was: "Motivation *is* Intelligence!"

Chapter 1

Needed: A Revolution in Learning

Technology and our human potential are the two greatest challenges and adventures facing humankind today.
—John Naisbitt, *Megatrends*[1]

It is often possible to discover change in the world through books. In my case, I had read a classic from the 1980s—*Megatrends*. It's a fascinating book because it hints at all the parts of our lives that will be influenced by technological change. The author of *Megatrends*, John Naisbitt, claimed that as we moved into a new information age, there would be a major impact on every aspect of modern-day life, work, and school. And it is true that computers and technology have most certainly infiltrated almost every aspect of our lives. However, in regard to teaching and learning, technology seems to have created an equally strong pressure against change. In fact, there are many people who really don't want technology to have a major impact on learning.

Specifically, everyone is aware that there is a special relationship that occurs between a teacher and a student. Many students have been especially impacted by a special teacher in their lives. Teaching and learning are two of the most primary connections people have with one another. Nobody really believes that technology could replace this powerful relationship between a student and teacher, and no one would ever want to break this important bond.

Yet, in many unpredictable ways, technology *is* encroaching upon teaching and learning. People are increasingly acquiring information from the Internet. They are viewing videos and instructional Web content in greater numbers, and they are spending exorbitant amounts of time playing video games and interacting through social media. While these activities may not be wholly considered "academic," their methods are so motivating that many educators are beginning to really take notice.

Strong motivation has always been considered a key reason for successful learning, but it can be woefully lacking within education, especially in the higher grades. So perhaps it could be possible for technology to provide a motivational component to learning, while also helping to meet the new learning challenges of the information age.

But what exactly are the challenges in the information age, and how are they impacting teaching and learning? According to *Megatrends*, it is really that excess information and complexity are being thrust upon us. Nesbitt notes that people are "drowning in information but starved for knowledge."[2,3] I can give a personal example of this. I remember when my kids were younger, we went to McDonalds to buy them a "Happy Meal." I was surprised to find a toy in the Happy Meal box that included not only batteries to install but also a small instruction manual!

All this made me realize that even the most commonplace devices today are amazingly complex. Nobody is really learning anything by trying to quickly get a happy meal toy up and running only to have it discarded or broken a few hours later. This is maddening! Within our daily lives, we are confronted with a bombardment of information that we process weakly. It seems that in the information age, there is a need for continuous but unstructured brainpower.

TECHNOLOGY ALLOWS FOR CONTROL

However, there can be one strong solution to the information overload program, and it is *control*. When people play specific video games of their interest, surf the Internet in a self-directed fashion, or interact with others through social media, they are in control what they are doing and learning. Having direct control over our learning can be a powerful step forward to combatting the information overload problem.

We all know that classroom learning does not, for the most part, provide any real control. The teacher and school district determine what is contained within the curriculum. With most computerized applications, however, the control of learning is with the user. They are free to choose what programs they want, skip to the topic or levels they require at that time, and pursue learning to the degree (deep or weak) that they feel is important to their needs.

In a sense it could be considered as a double-edged sword. Technology is making life more impersonal and complex, but technology is also providing the means to simplify this loss of personal connection and complexity. When control is introduced into the learning process, personal interest and meaning are included, which can be one of the most motivating things that people know. The important aspect to this fact is that knowledge and skills build on one another. It is not the random bits of information that are thrust upon us that are retained and utilized, but it is our specific and personalized knowledge which is built from ground up and continues to grow.

Unfortunately, this is not how public education is directed in this country. We, as a country, are pushing standardized learning to a larger degree in education. But, historically in America, there had been little standardized learning because curriculum had always been set locally. This had allowed teachers to align the content of their lessons to the specific interests and backgrounds of their students. In fact, the unique "openness" of the U.S. education system had frequently been cited as the reason it was always considered the best in the world. This fact was noted in one very interesting book, *The Race between Education and Technology*, by Claudia Goldin and Lawrence F. Katz. According to Goldin and Katz, the U.S. public education system was flexible enough to allow anyone to get ahead.

> If an open and forgiving system gave disadvantaged and errant youths a second chance, then the insistence on standards and accountability of many European systems reinforced a caste system. It is, in part, for these reasons that we deem the features of the U.S. educational system as virtues.[4]

In addition, Goldin and Katz state that an open and nonstandardized education system allowed for a better response to technological change.

> When technology advances rapidly, flexible, non-bureaucratic, decentralized institutions that are not beholden to a single funding authority are in a better position to respond. With the explosion of scientific fields in the post-world War II era, U.S. institutions were far better situated to adapt then were the more inflexible institutions in Europe.[5]

It is for these reasons that educators should begin to consider making—at least some components of—education *less* standardized instead of more standardized. The information age is exerting a large pressure on the educational community to adapt, and adapt it must do. We need technology in learning to allow teachers and students to have more choice and control in the learning environment.

FROM PEDAGOGY TO ANDRAGOGY

The role of formal education had always been to impart the important academic skills of the three Rs: reading, writing, and arithmetic. It had historically not been intended to teach the specific skills required for work or life. Malcolm Knowles (1913–1997), a pioneer and leader in the area of adult education, explained this notion when he pointed out the differences between *pedagogy*—the education of children, and *andragogy*—the training of adults.

Knowles created the term *andragogy* in the mid-1970s to bring attention to the fact that successfully training adults was an entirely different process than that of educating children—the word "pedagogy" itself starts with "ped," which means child. Knowles emphasized the word "training" for adults over the word "education." By doing this, he implied that the learning should be more tailored to the exact career objectives or life goals of the adult.

According to Knowles, pedagogy is centered on certain teaching techniques; it is focused on the fact that learners are mostly passive recipients of information, that their experiences outside of the educational environment are of little or no value, that the learners conform to a standardized curriculum, and that content be essentially of a theoretical nature.

Andragogy, on the other hand, requires that learners be active and interested participants in their learning, that they possess a rich storage of life experiences that can be used in the learning environment, that the curriculum be tailored to the needs and interests of the learners, and that content should emphasize applications that are both concrete and relevant to the learners' situation.[6]

In the industrial age (and before), the education of children and adults had always been different. Children went to school to learn basic knowledge and skills. After school ended, the students went their own way to learn what was required for "life's work." In today's world, however, students must begin to prepare for life's work before they finish high school, and there must be ways for them to continue to learn after high school has ended. It is generally agreed that a high school degree is no longer enough for students to gain and retain lifelong employment.

Although this increased need for knowledge and skills may seem overwhelming to many, as Nesbitt points out, the information age can be extremely liberating. In the past, individual circumstances were pretty much determined from birth. There was little upward mobility. If individuals were born to farmers, they generally became farmers. If they were born into poverty, they mostly stayed in those lower social classes. For today's generation of workers, knowledge and skills are the means to success, not class or circumstances. This makes, as Nesbitt says, "access to the economic system much easier."[7]

THE NEED FOR LIFELONG LEARNING

Previously, acquiring work skills entailed looking to the past to gain the techniques of farming or a trade. These same skills were passed down from generation to generation. Now, gaining and maintaining work skills requires peeking into the future as technology continually redefines the workplace.

In this case, modern education must be a cultivation of a standardized *and* an individualized set of knowledge and skills. In an increasingly diverse and competitive global workforce, a one-size-fits-all prescription for education achievement is no longer adequate.

Specifically, there must be a transformation from instruction that is only delivered to students in groups to some instruction that is delivered directly to the individual. In the new learning environment, learners must take a more active role in the learning process, and there must be more of a selection of learning opportunities from which they can partake.

Individualized learning must especially be a part of life after formal education. Training and re-training had traditionally been paid for by business or by the government, but in an increasingly competitive labor market, people need to be increasingly in charge of their own re-training. According to Richard Nelson Bolles, author of the massively best-selling book *What Color Is Your Parachute?*

> The important thing to remember now is that as large numbers of jobs are disappearing, "whole new categories of jobs are being created that nobody even thought of before," [For displaced workers] it is time to think harder about transferring the skills you have or acquiring new ones to move into a new type of job or industry. Be receptive to the idea that in the future you may be working "in the service of new technologies." With the right attitude, job seekers can often turn a crisis into a real advantage for themselves" by moving their life in a new and more fulfilling direction.[8]

It is true that the all-encompassing words within education reform today are accountability and standards, but I think the emphasis should be on a different word—motivation, because it can certainly be argued that when learners are motivated, especially older learners, many of the other achievement problems go away. Although not usually considered, motivation is a key component of successful learning for adolescents and adults, and it needs to be central to any learning plan to ensure lifelong learning.

As an example, the U.S. Army designed a computer game to enhance motivation. Faced with reducing enlistment, the army created a computer game to give prospective recruits a "feel" for army life. Called "America's Army," it was created to convey the substance of army life while also being exciting and challenging to play.

> Players go through basic training, advance to multiplayer games where they work in small units, and if they're successful, move on to become Green Berets. They rescue prisoners of war, protect a pipeline, and thwart a weapons scale to terrorists. Players earn points not only for killing enemies but also for protecting other soldiers and for completing a mission with everyone in the unit still alive.

If you try something stupid—for instance, gunning down civilians or ignoring orders—you can end up in a virtual Leavenworth prison or find yourself banished from the game altogether.[9]

When events are directly experienced, a positive feeling is produced in the brain's emotional (limbic) center, which causes learners to develop a positive attitude and subsequent increased motivation toward the event. Much evidence exists that "active" learning is more effective than "passive" learning and that it is far more meaningful and memorable.

MORE TECHNOLOGY FOR ADOLESCENTS AND ADULTS

Schools profess they teach to the individual but, in reality, academic success is really determined by how well a student does as compared to the group. It is a common phenomenon when some average students become outstanding leaders and innovators. It is sometimes the slower learners who show surprising success in areas such as artistic expression, entrepreneurial endeavors, and social leadership. Most likely this is because these abilities must be discovered and not necessarily taught or learned.

When children learn, their ways of learning are more similar than they are for adolescents and adults. Children do most of their learning in school, while older students increasingly direct their learning according to an area of interest or ability—whether it is in school or not. The same underachieving teenager who is doing poorly in school is, at home, composing music for a rock video, developing a website, or "hacking" into a computer system. Of course, these same types of real-world competencies can be easily simulated on a computer. They can challenge and excite the learner in new ways.

Modern society has largely been impacted by the advances in technology. These kinds of advances, however, have not occurred to the same extent within education. The primary reason for this is because teaching and learning are perceived to be distinctly human processes, and they cannot be easily duplicated through electronic means.

It is the intention of this book to present the case that teacher-student interaction may be vitally important for younger students, but it becomes less important for older students. By incorporating technology tools into the learning plan for adolescents and adults, it can gradually move them away from the standardized and dependent methods of pedagogy to the diverse and independent methods of andragogy.

Effective learning at the secondary level and beyond will occur only when each student's individual interests and abilities are taken into account, and when they have some control over their own learning. This is similar to how apprenticed tradesmen have learned work skills throughout the generations. When new information is presented according to real-world situations of relevance and interest, there is better learning.

The use of computerized learning is not intended to replace the traditional classroom setting; instead it is meant to be a complement to it, to enhance it, and to personalize it. After all, formal classroom learning has been around for at least a thousand years and has served us well. However, educational technology can make the educational experience more engaging, more relevant, and more useful to the "adult" needs of self-enhancement. This is important as the world moves increasingly into a knowledge society.

Before the Industrial Revolution, few people attended high school, and they were mostly functionally illiterate. The Industrial Revolution made high school necessary. People needed to learn new skills to live independently in this larger industrialized world. Today it can certainly be argued that with the information revolution we are also living in an even larger world—a globalized one.

Additionally, in this information age, a high school degree is no longer adequate; there needs to be postsecondary learning for everyone. But with the sheer amount of information exploding in all domains, this post high school learning must become specialized and self-directed.

Through technology, anyone can begin to have a diversification in their learning that will best meet their needs and goals for the future. Effective educational software can be used to improve on traditional academic subjects, introduce new ones, and promote lifelong learning by introducing some self-selection of material.

The most important point with adolescent and adult learners is that, as they grow older and more diverse, it becomes increasingly difficult and ineffective to teach them all in the same way in one classroom. Just as no single book will be enjoyed by every reader, no one learning event will be enjoyed or be effective with every learner. In addition to regular classroom learning, there can and should be individualized and self-directed technology-based learning for every student.

It is now time to explore the specific learning theories that will explain how technology can enhance learning. Technology, aligned with these psychological and adult learning principles, while also promoting individual control and motivation, can improve achievement for all older learners. This book will explain how.

CHAPTER 1—KEY POINTS TO REMEMBER

- Technology had traditionally not been utilized within education because teaching and learning are perceived to be uniquely human processes, but this is changing.

- Technology is impacting learning because it allows for control, which is highly motivating. It is a primary reason that web surfing, social networking, and video games are so popular, and educators have taken notice.
- Technology has changed the nature of work, and education must change in response. A more knowledgeable and skilled workforce is required, which can be aided through educational technology applications.
- A needed revolution in learning will incorporate individualized learning alongside traditional classroom approaches by blending pedagogic methods and andragogic methods.

NOTES

1. John Naisbitt, *Megatrends: Ten New Directions Transforming Our Lives*. New York: Warner Books, 1984 (pp. 35–52).

2. John Naisbitt, *Megatrends: Ten New Directions Transforming Our Lives*. New York: Warner Books, 1984 (pp. 35–52).

3. John Naisbitt, *Megatrends: Ten New Directions Transforming Our Lives*. New York: Warner Books, 1984 (p. 17).

4. Claudia Goldin and Lawrence F. Katz, *The Race between Education and Technology*. Cambridge, MA: The Belknap Press of Harvard University Press, 2008 (p. 132).

5. Claudia Goldin and Lawrence F. Katz, *The Race between Education and Technology*. Cambridge, MA: The Belknap Press of Harvard University Press, 2008 (p. 261).

6. M. S. Knowles, *The Modern Practice of Adult Education: From Pedagogy to Andragogy* (Rev. Ed.). Chicago, IL: Education Press, 1980.

7. John Naisbitt, *Megatrends: Ten New Directions Transforming Our Lives*. New York: Warner Books, 1984 (p. 9).

8. Phyllis Korkki, "The Economy Changes, So Change with It," *The New York Times*, April 20, 2008.

9. Daniel H. Pink, *A Whole New Mind: Why Right-Brainers Will Rule the World*. New York, NY: Riverhead Books, 2009 (p. 190).

Chapter 2

Using All of the Mind

The world is run by those who show up. Get involved.
—A bumper sticker

The brain can learn in three distinct ways—by acquiring academic *knowledge*, by absorbing sensory *experiences*, and by developing *skills*. To thrive, students should learn in these three very different ways. School learning, however, tends to focus primarily on only one learning type—the learning of academic knowledge.

It was the cognitive psychologist Endel Tulving (1927–present) who was first to determine that there are different memory types within long-term memory, called semantic, episodic, and procedural memories.[1] As noted in one book on learning:

> Any human activity requires three elements: knowledge to understand the context of the activity and predict outcomes; skills with which to act, and the attitude or motivation to act.[2]

When deep knowledge, meaningful experiences, and practical skills are all woven together in relevant ways, information is better understood, retained, and able to be applied in varied situations. And, it is in all three of these areas where educational technology can be used to improve learning.

IMPROVING SEMANTIC MEMORY

When specific facts and concepts are stored in the brain, it is usually referred to as knowledge. The prominent child psychologist Jean Piaget (1896–1980) studied extensively the process of knowledge acquisition. He determined that the process seems to change with age. Children first acquire knowledge in a general way and then expand to understand it in a more abstract way. In Piaget's studies, he noticed that students of the same age tended to make similar errors in their thinking (i.e., they thought that clay which had been rolled flat was actually bigger than when it was shaped as a ball). As most people are aware, a child does not see and understand the world in the same way that an adult does. A child learns about the physical world in a way that is more direct and "concrete." An adult, on the other hand, is capable of symbolic thinking and can understand the world based on abstract principles.

Piaget divided the knowledge development of the child into four stages: (1) sensori motor, (2) preoperational, (3) concrete operational, and (4) formal operational.[3] As a child progresses from one stage to the next, the cognitive structures of the preceding stage act as a foundation for the knowledge to be understood in the next stage. Piaget believed that these stages represented a single route of development for all students. He also frequently utilized the word *adaptation* in his theories to emphasize that a learner's knowledge mostly builds on knowledge that is adaptive in nature.

There is pretty substantial evidence across countries and cultures that children do pass through these stages. Given this evidence, there can certainly be strong merit to the argument that a standards-rich curriculum can be highly beneficial for younger students to ensure they proceed uniformly through these stages. However, this may not be the case for adolescents and adults. Piaget himself had very little to stay about the nature of the last stage of learning development, which is formal operations. And even currently, there continues to be much less study and thought about the formal operational stage or even agreement on whether all students actually reach this stage.

Because of the difficulty of clarifying the instructional needs of the formal operational stage, which generally occurs around the high school level, some individualized learning with technology may present the best way to address its varied nature. According to Piaget, there are two ways that the learning for older students will vary.

The first way is the *rate*. Some students will advance more quickly through school and will be able to handle more advanced work. Other students, on the other hand, will need additional time and instruction to keep up.

The second way that adult learning can vary is that it will increasingly reflect each learner's own "adaptive" nature. This means that underlying knowledge structures can be quite different between students depending on their background, culture, learning style, and other factors. In this regard, completing some technology-based instruction according to the student's unique learner characteristics can greatly benefit them. The way that knowledge learning can be aided by technology is explained in more detail in chapter 3.

IMPROVING EPISODIC MEMORY

It is both formal education *and* day-to-day experiences that contribute to a student's learning events. The outcomes of these "incidental" events can frequently alter the course of life and many times for the better. It is true that the most successful people in life are not afraid to try something new—they "get involved."

Providing students with enriching experiences has seldom been a priority of formal education. But when students experience something new, they can get a direct "feel" for it, which may become one of the most powerful motivating events they know. In the same way, the army used a video game to allow perspective recruits to get a feel for army life, a virtually unlimited number of experiences can be provided to students, so they can get a direct feel for them.

One very important aspect of episodic memory that Edwin Tulving noted was that people remember events chronologically. As each new experience is remembered, it becomes "stacked" in the front of a chronological organization like index cards in a box. This makes episodic memories much easier to retain. One only has to think about the specific time in their life to bring up the memory, and it means that episodic memories are the strongest memories that we have.

The strength of episodic memory implies that people can remember something best when they have directly experienced it. For example, I may be told that it is safe to eat red berries; yet in my past, I became ill from eating red berries. My personal experience of becoming ill from eating red berries will be remembered more clearly and be weighted more heavily in my decision making to eat red berries than any rule I hear.

Putting personal experiences over all other knowledge seems to be an adaptive quality because directly experiencing something tends to be the most reliable way to know it for certain. Psychologists call this process of weighing personal experience higher than acquired knowledge as a *computational bias*.[4]

Schools have always advocated the use of field trips for students to attend museums, historical sites, cultural events, etc., so they can directly experience what they are learning. One former teacher, John Taylor Gatto, author of the book *Weapons of Mass Instruction*, believes that experiences should be an essential part of education (i.e., students should visit a courtroom when learning about the law). In his book, he wrote:

> Back in the early 1940s, during World War II, I walked through the industrial river town of Monongahela, Pennsylvania several times a week at night, walked miles and miles with my mother, Bootie, and my sister Joanie.... We took

the last walk together around 1947. Beginning seven years later and continuing for years afterward, I attended five colleges, two of them Ivy League, but my degreed schooling proved to be a waste of time where intellectual development was concerned. I can't seem to recall a single thing I learned at those famous universities, Cornell and Columbia; not a single class, not a single teacher. Yet I remember everything about those walks down to the tiniest details.[5]

It is true that words alone cannot express the richness of a Beethoven symphony, sunset over water, or a peaceful moonlight swim. These events must be experienced. However, what can most easily be overlooked is that much what is experienced in the world comes from indirect, symbolic methods—through reading, television, or video/movies. After reading a book like *Treasure Island*, a reader can easily feel like they were standing right alongside the pirates during their conquests.

What is experienced through books, computers, and media can be just as effective as direct, in-person methods. A simulated activity on the computer can provide an enriching experience that is for the most part every bit as real as an actual event. Through the powerful effects of audio and visuals, students can experience events not always possible to them in other ways.

All sensations and experiences from the environment are, in fact, first filtered through the brain's emotional center, the limbic system. These sensations are then perceived as positive or negative leading them to acquire an emotional aspect. After undergoing a number of positive or negative experiences, people often develop certain attitudes about their experiences.

A deeply felt attitude can result in a more lasting type of learning than any other type. An appreciation for visual arts, for example, may long outlast the specifics of drawing. This is why people should be exposed to enriching experiences for no other reason than to "open their eyes" to what is possible in the world, and technology can provide the ways to do it. The way that experiential learning can be aided with technology is explained in more detail in chapter 4.

IMPROVING PROCEDURAL MEMORY

After accumulating a sufficient amount of knowledge, students can acquire skills for manipulating this knowledge in productive ways. It is true for the most part that knowledge is of little value if it cannot be converted into productive uses for society. "Skills of any kind are context and knowledge dependent—skills without knowledge are empty," as noted in one book on learning.[6]

After a foundation of knowledge is acquired, skills or procedural ability comes from continued practice. Once a person has learned how to ride a bike, they can "jump on" and confidently ride a bike for the rest of their lives.

A piano player will study the keys, notes, and rhythm, and then practice on the keyboard. Once a level of mastery is reached, piano players no longer have to read music or even look at their hands to guide them. The piano-playing procedure is in their heads, and it remains there permanently.

Benjamin Bloom (1913–1999), a prominent educational psychologist, studied procedural (skill)-based learning extensively. He conducted classic experiments on expert performers, which included Olympic swimmers, concert pianists, and research mathematicians. He determined that expert performers had similar characteristics. They had: (1) a strong motivation to practice, (2) a strong will to succeed, and (3) the ability to rapidly learn new techniques in their talent field.[7]

Repeatedly practicing skills leads to what Bloom called *automacity*—the capacity to perform without conscious attention. Once a skill has reached automacity, it requires frequent use but very little thought to maintain at that level. After achieving an automatic performance, other conscious brain functions can occur during the automatic functions—such as learning something new.

It is acquired cognitive skills that make one able to perform the tasks of daily work and life. These complex skills are increasingly needed in today's automated workplaces. They range from operating a piece of machinery to compiling a report. Unlike verbal information, cognitive skills cannot be learned by simply hearing or reading them. Cognitive skill learning requires the manipulation of knowledge for a particular purpose.

When employers hire workers, they look for education and work experience. They realize that academic learning does not always prepare a person for the kinds of tasks they must perform on the job. The ultimate question becomes: How can people learn complex cognitive skills when they have not yet had the opportunity to practice or use them?

Apprenticeships and internships are one way to expose students to important skills, but another way is through computerized learning. Interactive computer software can provide varied practice that will allow anyone to greatly enhance their skills. It can prepare them for the real world of work by simulating real-world tasks. As Allan Collins and Richard Halverson noted in *Rethinking Education in the Age of Technology*:

> We can imagine a day when most of the training that workers get for their jobs bypasses traditional educational institutions and takes place in online environments. Salespeople might practice their skills with simulations of recalcitrant customers. Doctors might practice their skills by trying to diagnose unusual

cases. Future travel agents might be challenged to develop cost-effective trip plans using the web. In fact, almost any job-related skill can be taught by practicing the skill, and computer simulations can create immersive environments where the target skills are necessary for solving engaging problems.[8]

As the workplace continually changes, people must stay on top of skill development to meet the requirements of new professions. They must often develop skills before they are able to use them. For example, after the Internet was created, a whole new array of technological skill necessity arose in the area of web page development. A few companies "started up" in order to offer those services, and many businesses had to pay large consulting fees to have their websites built. Now webpage building is a skill that many people possess. Those who quickly acquired the skills for webpage development stayed ahead of others and were able to capitalize on those proficiencies.

Obtaining cognitive skills means learning how to do something in a systematic manner. Students will need more opportunities to build their cognitive skills from simple to complex. With technology, they can practice skills at increasing levels of difficulty. The way that procedural learning can be aided with technology is explained in more detail in chapters 5 and 6.

WHAT IS INTELLIGENCE?

Since we are proposing that technology can greatly enhance adult learning, it is important to consider the nature of intelligence. Does intelligence exist outside of academic knowledge, or does intelligence grow based on that knowledge? If a student performs well on an achievement test, does this mean he or she is more intelligent than someone else, or just learned the material better? And what about the notion of "street smarts"? While some learners don't perform so well in academic settings, they do well in other aspects of life.

In 1927, a psychologist named Charles Spearman proposed that intelligence involves a very high degree of general ability. He called this a "g—(general) factor."[9] After he formulated his idea of a g-factor, intelligence tests soon were constructed to measure this general ability. These tests mostly consisted of items that measured for verbal and mathematical ability, and the tests turned out to be pretty good predictors of academic achievement. But questions always remained on whether the g-factor was the only component of intelligence.

The one definition of intelligence that has seemed to stand the test of time is that "intelligence is what intelligence tests measure." This sounds like a redundant, circular definition, but it does have some validity. It means that if a person is successful at tasks considered by society to require intelligence, then tests that reflect those tasks will serve as a measure of intelligence. This implies that intelligence is mostly categorized by the skills most prized by society, and as noted in one book on intelligence:

> Whatever the basic neurochemical mechanisms of cognition are, most psychologists would agree that the way intelligence is defined and manifested is culturally bound, affected by historical and social circumstances.[10]

Since verbal and mathematical abilities were always the ones most valued—at least in this modern age—they were deemed to be the most intelligent.

However, there are two interesting characteristics of the g-factor. The first is that it seems to be getting larger. IQ scores have shown quite substantial gains in the last half-century, and this has occurred in many countries as well as the United States.[11] This brings up the question: if g is a measure of a person's general intelligence, how can it be changing and getting larger?

The accepted reason for this growth is that as intelligent people have more access to enriching learning environments, they get even smarter. And it is true that schools are focusing more and more on improving verbal and mathematical abilities in their students. But the question posed by many is whether these abilities should be the only ones that are considered as "intelligent," as opposed to arts, music, mechanics, technical, etc.?

There is one other very interesting characteristic about the g-factor. While the g-factor tends to be a reliable predictor of academic success for children, it becomes a *less* accurate predictor for adults. Testing of the g-factor becomes less reliable as people age, and the very nature of intelligence seems to change as people get older.[12] It seems to be less focused on absorbing completely new knowledge, and instead, becomes more directed to acquiring what is adaptive to cope with work and life.

From Fluid to Crystallized Intelligence

Psychologist James M. Cattell (1860–1944) formulated a theory of intelligence to explain how this developmental change in intelligence occurs: fluid vs. crystallized intelligence. Fluid intelligence consists of "g," the general factor of intelligence, and includes all of the abilities required for formal education. Crystallized intelligence, in contrast, reflects the skills acquired from both formal education and *from living*. As a person ages, they decline in fluid intelligence, but they gain in crystallized intelligence.

According to Cattell, fluid intelligence tends to peak during adolescence and then declines in adulthood. Crystallized intelligence, on the other hand, continues to increase throughout adulthood. Crystallized intelligence improves as individuals continue to be "information seeking."[13] That is, they attempt to seek out what knowledge and skills are most beneficial to them.

While children may thrive when learning general knowledge, adults tend to learn best when the learning is more directly targeted to meeting their needs and goals. As Cattell noted, the two types of intelligence are both vitally important. Fluid intelligence is required for creating a base of knowledge required for life in society. Crystallized intelligence, on the other hand, is necessary for the acquisition of practical knowledge so a person can perform competently in their daily work and life.

Targeting learning activities for older learners that better supports their day-to-day situations is a more natural and comfortable way for them to learn. Educational technology can be an ideal way to bring this real-world and purposeful learning to adults.

The Multifactor or Aptitudes

Many psychologists, including Howard Gardner of Harvard University, have advocated that people do not have one form of intelligence, but more than one—seven different kinds—according to Gardner. It is true that in adolescence and adulthood, it becomes obvious that some students seem to have a superiority in some areas as opposed to others.

One student is a wiz in arithmetic but has a difficulty with writing. Another student is a "natural" when working with mechanical devices but is a poor reader. A third student has an "ear" for music but doesn't do especially well in academic subjects. These students are functioning in different ways—mentally. As they continue through life, they will grow farther apart in their ways of thinking and learning.

Although rarely emphasized within academic settings, people should be able to determine their natural abilities or "aptitudes," so as to make the best choices for career and life. Discovering aptitudes may be a whole new way to improve learning as one book about intelligence explains:

> Intelligence always manifests itself as an interaction between underlying intellectual abilities and experiences in particular domains and is therefore context/content dependent. [Furthermore,] multiple intelligences exist, and IQ tests measure only a specific type of intelligence, namely one developed in academic settings.[14]

In addition, the psychologist Benjamin Bloom had this to say about the nature of intelligence.

> Benjamin Bloom has found that if instead of relying on a single IQ score, when use is made of tests like Thurstone's seven primary mental abilities, as much as 50 percent of the population is gifted in one or more areas.[15]

Standardized tests produce an estimate of a student's general level of academic achievement, but they generally do little to determine natural abilities.

Realizing Adaptation and "Street-Smarts"

Psychologist Robert Sternberg (1949–present) created the term "street-smarts" with the intent to explain the abilities contained in one part of his three-part theory of intelligence called the *practical*. According to Sternberg, the practical part of intelligence is always associated with relevant, real-life situations.

> Practical intelligence is the ability to adapt to everyday life by drawing on existing knowledge and skills. Practical intelligence enables an individual to understand what needs to be done in a specific setting and then do it.[16]

What Sternberg is really saying is that a large part of intelligence is the ability to adapt. Adaptive learning is rarely emphasized in formal education, but it is becoming increasingly important as the world of work continuously changes. Once students identify their abilities, they will be better able to understand themselves, make the best career choices, and determine ways to direct their abilities as needed. It allows them to find a "goodness of fit" for themselves and in their lives.

Adaptive abilities are best determined when novel situations challenge a student's capabilities, rather than the mostly routine situations of the classroom. Successful people in general are able to find ways to make the most of their strengths while also compensating for their weaknesses. After people recognize their adaptive capabilities, they can develop what has been called adaptive expertise.[17] One well-known story can illustrate adaptive expertise quite well. It is the epic tale of *Gone with the Wind*. In this story, it is Scarlet O'Hara and Rhett Butler who have the most adaptive expertise. They are able to find ways to adapt and even thrive within the chaotic post–Civil War South. Other characters in the story are less able to adjust to their new lives and do not achieve as much. Many of these characters, such as Ashley Wilkes, are considered much more "intelligent" than Scarlett O'Hara and Rhett Butler. Real-world or adaptive ability is a very important component to a successful life.

It is true that some highly intelligent students can have difficulty in the world outside the classroom while other students who performed poorer academically end up doing pretty well. These less than academically successful people are able to develop specific competencies that allow them to become productive in life.

Individual aptitudes usually manifest themselves in early adulthood. As each learner becomes more aware of their strengths and weaknesses, they can begin to utilize technology applications to address them. Educational technology can help people become smarter both academically and adaptively.

CHAPTER 2—KEY POINTS TO REMEMBER

- The mind stores information in three ways: semantic (memory for knowledge), episodic (memory for experiences), and procedural (memory for skills), but schools have mostly instructed to semantic memory, leaving the other memories underutilized.
- Piaget determined that knowledge (contained in semantic memory) is learned in stages. The final stage of formal operations, occurring around adolescence, is more varied and would benefit from individualized learning.
- Episodic memory consists of specific events and is the most lasting memory we have. Incorporating more sensory learning can better engage students, and "open their eyes to possibilities in the world."
- Procedural memory is for steps in a process. It required practice to create automaticity. Many technology apps exist that can increase practice of skills.
- Children learn through fluid intelligence which is more general, while adolescents and adults learn through crystalized intelligence, which is more specific to real life. In addition, there is evidence of multiple-intelligences, and individual aptitudes can develop as students grow older. These factors can make individualized learning more beneficial for older learners.

NOTES

1. Adam Cash, Ph.D., *Psychology for Dummies: A Reference for the Rest of Us*. Indianapolis, IN: Wiley Publishing, Inc., 2002 (p. 142). A good book to review classic psychology principles and studies.
2. Edited by Maurice Holt, *Skills and Vocationalism, The Easy Answer*. Philadelphia, PA: Open University Press, 1987 (p. 26).
3. J. Piaget, *The Psychology of Intelligence*. Totowa, NY: Littlefield, Adams, 1972.
4. Keith E. Stanovich, "The Fundamental Computational Biases of Human Cognition," The *Psychology of Problem Solving*, Cambridge: Cambridge University Press, 2008 (p. 313).
5. John Taylor Gatto, *Weapons of Mass Instruction: A Schoolteacher's Journey through the Dark World of Compulsory Schooling*. Gabriola Island, BC, Canada: New Society Publishers, 2009 (p. 59).
6. Maurice Holt (Ed.), *Skills and Vocationalism, The Easy Answer*. Philadelphia, PA: Open University Press, 1987 (p. 29).
7. B.S. Bloom, "The Hands and Feet of Genius," *Educational Leadership*, 43(5), 1986 (p. 70–77).
8. Allan Collins and Richard Halverson, *Rethinking Education in the Age of Technology: The Digital Revolution and Schooling in America*, New York, NY: Teachers College Press, 2009 (p. 74).

9. E. G. Boring, "Intelligence Is as the Tests Test It," *New Republic*, 35, 1923 (pp. 35–36).

10. Mike Rose, *Why School? Reclaiming Education for All of Us*, New York: The New Press, 2009 (p. 70).

11. Daniel T. Willingham, *Why Don't Students Like School: A Cognitive Scientist Answers Questions about how the Mind Works and What It Means in the Classsroom*, San Francisco, CA: Jossey-Bass, 2009 (pp. 136–137).

12. I. G. Humphreys and T. C. Davey, "Continuity in Intellectual Growth from 12 Months to 9 Years," *Intelligence* 12(2), 1988 (pp. 183–197).

13. M.S. Knowles, *Adult Development and Learning: A Handbook on Intellectual Growth and Competence in the Adult Years for Education and the Helping Professions*, San Francisco, CA: Jossey Bass, 1977.

14. Dorit Wenke and Peter A. Frensch, "Is Success or Failure at Solving Complex Problems Related to Intellectual Ability," *The Psychology of Problem Solving*, Cambridge, MA: Cambridge University Press, 2008 (p. 103).

15. Fenton Keys, *Exploring Careers for the Gifted*, New York: Richards Rosen Press Inc., 1981 (p. 12).

16. R. J. Sternberg, "A Contextualist View of the Nature of Intelligence," in P. S. Fry (Ed.), *Changing Conceptions of Intelligence and Intellectual Functioning: Current Theory and Research*, Oxford: North-Holland, 1984.

17. National Academy of Sciences, *How People Learn: Brain, Mind, Experience, and School*, Washington, DC: National Academy Press, 2000 (p. 73).

Chapter 3

Enhancing Knowledge Development

> *The real environment is altogether too big, too complex, and too fleeting for direct acquaintance. Men must make maps of the world.*
> —Walter Littman

Facts and concepts are the basic building blocks of knowledge, and both can be enhanced through technology. However, while facts can easily be learned through memorization, concepts cannot be learned this way. A concept must be learned at a greater depth to be truly known. A concept, as it is defined by the dictionary, is "a notion, thought or idea." For example, the philosopher Rene Descartes explained how the mind begins to understand the concept of "wax":

> At a particular time, my senses inform me of a shape, color, hardness, taste that belong to the wax. But at another time my senses inform me of a different shape etc. belonging to the wax. My senses show me nothing but the "sensory qualities" since my senses take them in. I nevertheless make a judgment of identity; it is the same piece of wax on the earlier and the later occasion. So, it is the nature of the ball of wax that it can possess different sensory qualities at different times. So, to understand what the wax is, I must use my understanding, not my senses.[1]

Since conceptual learning is the basis for mostly all higher-order thinking, it is important that students learn key concepts fully and completely. There are a number of ways that conceptual learning can be enhanced and reinforced through technology.

BETTER CONCEPTUAL LEARNING

Concepts are usually learned according to their attributes. For example, the concept of a mammal will have these attributes: it is warm blooded and provides milk for its young. Having students learn a concept's attributes can work well for basic concepts, but as concepts become more abstract, it can be more difficult for students to understand them. When learning complex concepts like "democracy" or "altruism," the learning should be done in a variety of ways so the attributes can be learned at greater depth.

The early educational psychologist E. L. Thorndike (1874–1949) said that when first learning a complex concept, at least thirty exposures are required before a learner knows it "cold."[2] Considering that highly educated people often cannot completely come to agreement on what a term like "democracy" means, thirty exposes may actually be the minimum!

The greater and more varied the ways that a concept's attributes are explained or experienced, the more likely the concept will be understood and retained. Educational technology is one way to expose learners to concept attributes in a variety of methods. For example, it is a common practice to simulate the founding fathers in order to understand democracy. When students are "role-playing" the founding fathers, they are actively constructing their ideas. As stated in one book on innovation within learning and education, it is important for students to move beyond simply being introduced to concepts to truly analyzing and mentally manipulating them.

> Critical thinking is the intellectually disciplined process of actively and skillfully conceptualizing, applying, analyzing, synthesizing, and/or evaluating information gathered from, or generated by, observation, experience, reflection, reasoning, or communication, as a guide to belief and action.[3]

Having students move to the higher levels of conceptional understanding requires many and different kinds of exposures. In this way, students can incorporate the information to produce something that is tangible and potentially new. Using a tool like a graphic organizer is a great way for students to clarify and organize the attributes of a complex concept. They can then use the attributes as the basis for a project utilizing technology. As also stated in the book on innovation in learning:

> Graphic organizers, like the Lotus Blossom, help students record their ideas in an organized manner—Venn Diagrams, fishbone, sequence organizers, compare-and-contrast, concept maps and more. Some websites offer free printable graphic organizers.[4]

This is why deep conceptual learning should be central to most subject areas. The objective is really to get closer and closer to a clearer meaning.

There is another way that complex concepts can be learned, and it is through association. This means that if students can associate a new concept with something they already know, the new information can be better understood and assimilated.

I can remember a case of my own initial understanding of a complex concept coming through an association. It was in the mid-1990s and I was sitting at a table in the lunchroom of my workplace. A few people at the table were talking about this new thing called the "Internet." I had been hearing people talk about the Internet, but I was having difficulty understanding exactly what the Internet was.

I finally got enough courage to speak up and asked: "What exactly is the Internet?" One of my co-workers replied. "It works through the phone system and is similar to how a telephone works. You use a code to 'call up' a website." Once I had an associated idea of the Internet working like the phone system, I immediately grasped the concept. All my subsequent knowledge of the Internet was built on this initial association.

As an example, a video game called *Stats Invaders* was created to support the understanding of statistical principles, usually very difficult for students.

> Players shoot at descending aliens in the style of old arcade games. The aliens fall according to a horizontal statistical distribution (e.g. they are more likely to descend in some locations than in others). To end a round, players have to set a bomb tuned to the frequency of the "mother ship" by picking which of the shapes on the right side best describes the shape of the ship dropping the aliens. The goal is to help students develop understanding about patterns within chance.[5]

Once students are allowed to "see" how a statistical distribution works, it becomes easier for them to understand it. The effectiveness of this game was tested on two groups of community college students. After both groups took a pretest on statistics, a first group of students read a short passage on patterns in randomness. Next, a second group of students read this same passage but also played the video game.

Results on a post-test showed that students from both groups learned from the written passage, but students in the gameplay condition learned much more than students in the no-gameplay condition. The game players were able to relate what they were reading to their recent experiences playing the game.[6]

BETTER ORGANIZATION OF KNOWLEDGE

Once students have acquired a strong base of concepts, they will become even better at grasping and retaining new related information. It is true that experts do not only know more in their area of expertise, but their knowledge is better organized, and it is easier for them to retrieve.

Evidence strongly supports this notion that experts organize their knowledge around the important concepts in their fields. For example, studies of chess experts showed that they can memorize whole chess board configurations when the configurations reflect a meaningful chess game. However, when chess boards were presented to chess experts in a random fashion, they could not remember any more pieces than novice players. This implied that chess experts remembered chess boards according to the strategic positions of pieces.

Research on physics experts have showed that they cited major physics principles or laws when asked how they would go about solving a physics problem. Physics novices, on the other hand, did not generally refer to major physics principles, but instead to common equations. This led to the conclusion that physics experts organized their knowledge around the "big ideas" in physics.

Studies in the area of mathematics showed that math experts always attempted to analyze the math problems to which they were presented, rather than simply plugging numbers into formulas. This implied that math experts centered their knowledge around particular problem types and what was required to solve those problems. Math novices, in contrast, applied general equations to math problems even when they weren't effective toward solving the problems.[7]

Most students will never reach these levels of expertise in their studies. However, all students can benefit from getting a clearer understanding of important concepts. When students view a variety of technology applications to accompany classroom learning, they can gain a greater understanding of the concepts.

MEETING LEARNER CHARACTERISTICS

Learner diversity becomes a greater problem as students grow older because their knowledge structures will increasingly begin to vary. This student diversity can encompass a large range of characteristics, and it is greatly affecting education today because the United States is becoming more of a diverse nation. As noted in a book on designing learning:

> The fewer the similarities of students, the more necessary it will be to provide individualized instruction since students are likely to be quite different from one another in what they can do when they enter. They can progress as a group if they are very similar in background and skills.[8]

Technology can be the key way to tackle this diversity because it can be targeted individually to the different learner characteristics. There are three primary areas of learner characteristics readiness to learn, cultural background, and learner rate and style.

Readiness to Learn

Readiness to learn is a learner characteristic that relates to having the appropriate prerequisite knowledge. As students grow older, their readiness levels will begin to vary more and more depending on their prior schooling and background. Learners with a more privileged upbringing will generally have more readiness to learn than others. Computerized learning is one way to level the playing field for underachievers, especially in the key academic areas of math and English language arts.

When students' readiness levels are weak, they can benefit from the help of a *structured learning environment*. Also called "scaffolding," computer-assisted instruction (CAI) tends to outline and organize information in a structured fashion. Direct practice with feedback is also provided with each segment of new information. Besides a general scaffolding of instruction, computerized learning utilizes many *cues* before, during, and after the learning. Adding tips, hints, visuals, and examples all help learning.[9]

When students' basic background knowledge is weak, their learning can benefit highly from a learning environment where the main concepts are clearly outlined for them. Tutorials and other CAI programs are ideal for providing new knowledge in a highly organized fashion that will benefit learners with weaker background knowledge and underachievers. It can help assure that there is a consistent readiness level.

Cultural Background

Another important learner characteristic is the culture or community in which a person lives. A student will have a strong knowledge structure based on their upbringing and cultural surroundings. This is because more time is spent around family and community than in any other place, including school.

When new learning does not fit in with a student's cultural or ethnic background, it cannot be well assimilated. This means that in some cases, outside knowledge will need to be modified or corrected. One Seattle newspaper article illustrated the problem of cultural diversity. This article noted what a panel of experts had to say to professional educators about the current state of education for one group of minority students—Native Americans:

> Dropout rates for minority students, especially Native Americans, are at crisis levels in six Northwestern states. After years of talking about how students need to be properly prepared for school, the panel said, *"it's time for schools to start preparing for students."* This is when Native American children first come in contact with "foreign cultures."[10] (emphasis added)

Providing a variety of learning activities including learning through technology can allow students from diverse cultural backgrounds to find learning events in which they feel the most comfortable. For example, Spanish-speaking students can take a math tutorial in Spanish. It will show them that instruction was designed by keeping them in mind.

I am easily reminded of the *Welcome Back, Kottier* series from the 1970s. Gabe Kottier was an effective teacher to the underachieving, "sweat hogs" in his classroom because he had grown up within the same community. He was able to relate to these students in a way that no one else could.

Instructional software can provide these same benefits if it is developed by those who have an intimate understanding of the community for which they are designing the software. And the software can be particularly successful for those learners who are members of that community. There should be choices for all educators in what applications they use.

Learner Rate and Style

A final area of learner characteristics is rate and style of learning. In the case of learning rate, one way of looking at it is through a computer analogy. Computers are often judged by their processing speed, but a computer with a slower processing chip is not "stupider" than a higher-end model with a faster processing chip; it just takes longer to do the work. Similarly, "slow learners" can process information as well as learners who are considered average or even above-average, but they will need more time and potentially more instruction.

Assuming that they have no major mental impairment, most students have the ability to do most academic tasks. Some may accomplish them faster, but all should eventually reach the same results. The decades of ranking students have really created an intellectual "social class." Some people are labeled as "smart," and others are labeled as "average" or "dull." Learning in a self-paced approach, like CAI and tutorials, can provide the variation of speed and practice required for slower learners.

The difference in learner rate is a further problem because it draws attention to those who appear to be "smarter" or "dumber" than others. This is why some learning needs to be done autonomously to avoid stigmatizing those that are taking longer to achieve a level of competency.

Once slower learners are aware that their inability is not due to being less intelligent but is mostly due to a lack of prior knowledge, time, and practice, they will achieve the self-confidence and motivation needed to continue to perform at the highest levels.

A final learner characteristic is often called learning style. Learning style refers to determining the best method by which a student can learn. Some learn best by reading or studying, while others learn best by doing. When people in general go about their day-to-day activities, they act in fairly consistent ways. This style of behaving is frequently referred to as a *cognitive style*.

Cognitive styles have been defined as "differences in preferences for perceiving, organizing and processing information." If a student doesn't particularly enjoy reading, they will not be able to get much from a reading activity. In this regard, there should be activities which allow for learning in a variety of ways.

I can provide an example of learning styles from my own work experience. I once designed two training courses for a newspaper company. The first course was intended to teach the graphic arts department how to use Adobe Quark Express, a desktop publishing software program. The second course was intended to teach the accounting department how to use Microsoft Excel, an accounting spreadsheet software program.

When the course was introduced to the first two groups of students, it quickly became apparent that the two student groups had very different learning styles. The graphic arts students, perhaps being more artistic, wanted a flexible course that allowed for a lot of time to "play" around with the software so they could best get an idea of its capabilities for their artistic expression.

In contrast, the accounting group, perhaps being more analytic, wanted to learn by a step-by-step process that clearly specified the exact procedures necessary to perform a specific accounting function. The end result was that both courses had to be redesigned so as to make the Quark Express course more general and exploratory and the Excel course more specific and sequential.

It is important to note, however, that the notion of learning styles has been controversial. Research has not found any support for different learning styles. Studies of different teaching techniques, that is, visual vs. auditory, have not shown any benefits to learners.[11,12] It is also important to point out, however, that all of the studies on learning styles—that I've seen—were done on children. As noted abundantly in this book, children and adults do not learn the same. Children have brains that are not fully developed.

Common sense also tells us that people seem to display different cognitive strengths and weaknesses. They also tend to work in fields related to their cognitive strengths. Some have a "head for numbers," for example. Students should have opportunities, through applications and projects, to determine which ways to learn are the most appealing to them.

STANDARDS ARE LIMITING

Given all of these variations in learner characteristics, does it make sense to continue the all-encompassing drive to standardize all curriculums in this country, especially at the high school level and beyond?

In today's complex and ever-changing technological society, tying academic goals solely to standards is most certainly too limiting. As Diane Ravitch noted in her book, *The Death and Life of the Great American School System*, education reform efforts centered on standards and testing have not been very successful:

> The reform movement inspired by the *Nation at Risk* report was raising standards and was working well for about a quarter of students; the successful students were the ones "who are able to learn in a traditional system, who are able to sit still, who are able to keep quiet, who are able to remember after they listened to someone else talk for five hours, who are able to pick up a book and learn from it—who've got all those things going for them." But the old ways were not working for the majority of kids.[13]

It is an unfortunate fact, and one that is frequently cited, that many extremely successful people dropped out of high school or college. Often these people had high aptitudes and a strong will to succeed in a particular area of interest and wanted to proceed more quickly and in depth than what they were experiencing in school. Most chose to do this on their own. As noted in one book on innovation in learning:

> Forcing students to master the same curriculum essentially discriminates against talents that are not consistent with the prescribed knowledge and skills. Students who are otherwise talented but do not do well in the prescribed subjects are often sent to spend more time on the core subjects, retained for another grade, or deprived of the opportunity to develop their talents in other ways.[14]

Bill Gates is one college dropout whose education was most definitely not standardized. He attended a special secondary school that was focused on a hands-on assembly and manipulation of computer components. He has credited this special school for his eventual building of a personal computer and then starting a company as a result. The important point is that learners need to be able to explore areas of interest and ability.

Many other talented individuals have had adverse circumstances in their lives that prevented them from applying themselves within the highly organized classroom setting. Their poor and immature behavior was held against them and masked their true abilities. One such student was Jim Clark, an entrepreneur who founded two extremely successful Silicon Valley companies Silicon Graphics and Netscape. The following section comes from a biography of Jim Clark:

> His father abandoned the family when Clark was a small child. He'd been an indifferent student and a cutup. The offense that got Clark tossed out for good

[in his junior year] was telling an English teacher to "go to hell." Once he left school—or school left him—he fled town.

At the minimum age of seventeen and a half, Clark asked his mother to sign the piece of paper that permitted him to join the Navy. [When in the Navy], he took his first math test and scored the highest grade in the class. He was unaware that he had any particular aptitude for math and didn't quite believe the result. Neither did anyone else. The Navy gave him another test. Same result.

Six weeks later Clark was assigned to teach basic algebra to incoming recruits. A few after that, one of his instructors told him that it had been a long time since he'd seen someone so naturally gifted in mathematics. He suggested that Clark enroll in night classes at Tulane University with a view of getting a college degree after he'd finished his tour of duty. Within eight years Clark had his college degree, plus a Master's in Physics, plus a Ph.D. in Computer Science.[15]

It is most likely that most students are not being able to actualize their abilities and interests. Computerized learning can challenge and excite those learners who for whatever reasons are not being reached in traditional ways. New methods for knowledge development must be available, especially to those who have been low achievers, so they can find ways to become successful.

CHAPTER 3—KEY POINTS TO REMEMBER

- A concept is the smallest building block of knowledge. While simple concepts can be learned through attributes or associations, more complex concepts will require exposure to multiple cases for students to master.
- The learning of knowledge occurs best when it is in context and when it can be associated to what we already know. Expert knowledge is highly organized, allowing experts to absorb new related knowledge more rapidly. For students without such background knowledge, they will usually require a structured learning environment, such as what a tutorial can provide, to guide them through the learning process.
- Learner characteristics encompass learner readiness, background, rate, and style. These variables become more diverse as students grow older and can best be addressed through individualized learning.
- There is a greater push to standardize curriculums in schools, but standardized learning can be limiting and demotivating for older learners. Some individualized learning alongside standardized learning can better meet the needs of older learners.

NOTES

1. Simon Blackburn, *Think: A Compelling Introduction to Philosophy*. New York: Oxford Press, 1999 (p. 31).
2. E. L. Thorndike, *Education: A First Book*, New York: Macmillan, 1912.
3. Sharron "Sam" Sakai-Miller, *Innovation Age Learning—Empowering Students by Empowering Teachers*. Arlington, VA: ISTE, 2016 (p. 114).
4. Sharron "Sam" Sakai-Miller, *Innovation Age Learning—Empowering Students by Empowering Teachers*. Arlington, VA: ISTE, 2016 (p. 116).
5. Daniel L. Schwartz and Dylan Arena, *Measuring What Matters Most: Choice-Based Assessments for the Digital Age*. Cambridge MA: MIT Press, 2013 (p. 61).
6. F. C. Bartlett, *Remembering*. Cambridge, MA: Cambridge University Press, 1932.
7. National Academy of Sciences, *How People Learn: Brain, Mind, Experience, and School*. Washington, DC: National Academy Press, 2000 (pp. 32–35).
8. Robert Frank Mager and Kenneth M. Beach, *Developing Vocational Instruction*, Delmont, CA: Pitman Learning, Inc., 1967 (p. 35).
9. F. I. M. Craik and J. C. Rabinowitz, "Age Differences in the Acquisition of Use of Verbal Information," In J. Long and A. Baddeley (Eds.), *Attention and Performance*, vol. 10. Hillsdale, NJ: Erlbaum, 1984.
10. Seattle Associated Press, "Minority Students High School Dropout Rates Reach 'Crisis Levels'" June 2, 2008.
11. Todd I. Lubart and Christophe Mouchiround, "Creativity: A Source of Difficulty in Problem Solving," *The Psychology of Problem Solving*. Cambridge, MA: Cambridge University Press, 2008 (p. 130).
12. Daniel T. Willingham, *Why Don't Students Like School: A Cognitive Scientists Answers Questions about How the Mind Works and What It Means for Your Classroom*. San Francisco, CA: Jossey-Bass, 2009.
13. Diane Ravitch, *The Death and Life of the Great American School System: How Testing and Choice Are Undermining Education*. New York, NY: Basic Books, 2010 (p. 122).
14. Sharron "Sam" Sakai-Miller, *Innovation Age Learning—Empowering Students by Empowering Teachers*. USA: ISTE, 2016 (p. 14).
15. Michael Lewis, *The New New Thing—A Silicon Valley Story*. New York, NY: W.W. Norton & Company, Inc. 2000 (pp. 45–46).

Chapter 4

Providing for Experience—It's the Best Teacher

A "classic" is a book that everybody praises but nobody reads.
—Mark Twain

Students' earliest learning begins through meaningful experiences, and powerful experiences usually comprise their most vivid memories. This is why learning through experiences can provide the most lasting and impactful learning that students encounter. Providing actual experiences is not always possible for every student. Providing them through real-world learning on a computer is possible for everyone.

In a diverse society like the United States, many students do not have the opportunity to be exposed to consistent meaningful experiences that can lead them to a happy and productive life. In most cases, learning directly through the senses has not been emphasized within formal education. But older learners need exposure to a wide variety of real-world experiences to augment their learning, and especially to show them examples of good cases.

BETTER LEARNING THROUGH THE SENSES

When thinking about a word or idea, an image usually comes to mind. This is referred to as "seeing in the mind." It has long been known that the earliest forms of learning are in two forms—visual and auditory.[1] The child psychologist Jean Piaget noted that the first instances of "cognition" occur in babies around the age of one year to eighteen months.

At this time they develop object permanence, which is the ability to remember that an object exists outside of immediate sight. The child has then developed a visual memory of a toy, person, or other object in the world. In a similar way that newborn babies gain initial understanding of the world through the senses, all learners acquire most of their initial understanding this way. When students are able to visualize information, they can gain a clearer understanding.

As schoolwork, the workplace, and the world in general become more complex, the average student must learn at a higher degree to function successfully, and this can more easily be done when some information is presented through visuals and media. It must be recognized that if students are to stay in school longer and to learn much more complex and abstract information, there must be ways to make the learning easier, at least initially.

John Amos Comenius (1592–1670), a prominent educator and early champion of universal education, was the first person to advocate using pictures in textbooks. Now few people could even imagine making a textbook without pictures, as learners would have a hard time understanding new knowledge without at least some of the information shown through a diagram or picture. Technology today can take the next step.

GOING FROM PICTURES TO WORDS TO PICTURES AGAIN

The written word is a relatively recent addition to humanity. It has only been in the last 500 years that people have communicated through words. For the previous 10,000 years, people communicated primarily through images. Early writing methods such as hieroglyphics and pictographs are very similar to the object portrayed, such as a circle with lines pointing outward to depict the sun. Over time, communication evolved to a highly abstract written form.

By the nineteenth century, speaking with formal language became a prerequisite for wealth, status, and power. A precisely crafted sentence structure was directed at all prose. When considering speeches by people such as Abraham Lincoln, it is easy to recognize the complexity in the writing. Today, the opposite is becoming true. There is a movement away from formal language and an emphasis instead on language that is similar to the way it is commonly spoken.

Many people believe that this "easier" language was introduced by America's favorite writer, Mark Twain. Mark Twain made a critical decision to make Huck Finn the narrator of the tale Huckleberry Finn. This book offended many when it was first published because it allowed everyone into the "head" of the main character, so they could understand his feelings instead of trying to interpret them from a second-person narrative. The story was also presented in the vernacular (slang) of the character.

Digital media is taking this transformation from complex verbal communication to a much simpler form of communication a step further. It is changing communication from verbal to mostly visual-auditory. For example, in movies today, a character usually speaks no more than three or four sentences before the next character speaks. Today's movies are "scripted" for visual and auditory impact, not words.

USING MEDIA TO ENHANCE LEARNING

Learning and understanding through the senses has often been the basis for creativity and has led to major discoveries in fields such as medicine, mathematics, and biology. For example, Einstein developed his theory of relativity by imagining himself riding on a beam of light. Only then could he conceptualize that light could have the properties of both particles and waves.

Software companies regularly point out to their customers how much easier their products are to use when they contain graphics. After the graphic user interface was first introduced on the Macintosh screen, it quickly became the standard for PC interface design. In fact, the entire field of graphic arts is expanding as people realize "a picture *is* worth a thousand words."

> The fact that charts, diagrams, schematics, and spread sheets are very useful ways to display information has been quickly understood by IBM and Apple. These companies waste no time pointing out to prospective customers how much more useable and salable their products are due to their use of graphics. In this respect, they are far ahead of most educators.[2]

In the future, effective communication will increasingly consist of the ability to convey information simply and accurately to a larger and more diverse audience. Often referred to as "media literacy," this new form of communication style emphasizes conveying information in additional ways besides print.

> Media literacy is the medium of delivering messages (print, graphics, animation, audio, video, Web sites, and so on), the crafting of the message for a particular medium, the graphic "look and feel" of a Web site, for example, and the impacts that the media message has on its audience.[3]

It is true that the attention of students is increasingly being taken away from talking instructors, and from the routineness of the classroom. Instead, it is being pulled to the engaging environment of media. There is a common belief among educators that viewing media quite literally scrambles the mind, but the fact is that the evolution from verbal to visual-auditory is here, and it is accelerating. When determining how students gain information, from television, the Internet, and movies/video, it is unrealistic to believe they are going to want to learn solely by listening to lectures or reading books.

But media has the capacity to ignite learning when otherwise there has been little or none. Media can provide an answer to the problem of conveying information that has become too complex, too abstract, or, in some cases, too dull by conventional means. Providing certain amounts of knowledge through media can build a foundation for a larger and more sustained knowledge base. In most cases, knowledge builds on images. If students cannot clearly "see" what they are learning, they will not have a clear understanding.[4]

SESAME STREET—MEDIA IN LEARNING

Sesame Street is probably the first instance of using media in learning. Although it is a program for children, much can be learned from the *Sesame Street* TV series to improve learning for older students. Even today, after forty years, *Sesame Street* has retained its popularity and continues to help prepare children for school. According to a *USA Today* article on the fortieth anniversary of *Sesame Street*, "it is indisputably the most beloved children's show in history and one of television's biggest and most enduring success stories."[5]

The key factor for *Sesame Street*'s effectiveness is its specific design for children. It makes learning meaningful by incorporating features they know and love. Children like *Sesame Street*'s humor, music, puppets, and stories. Early developers of *Sesame Street* were in agreement with the notion that learning could not occur if children were not paying close enough attention to the content. The entertainment value of *Sesame Street* increased its instructional effectiveness because children were attending to it at a greater degree.

Sesame Street developers spent a great amount of time redesigning the program according to the results of their vigorous testing based on the attention level of the children. Multiple studies have indicated that *Sesame Street* continues to produce positive results for school readiness in children.

> Researchers at the University of Massachusetts and the University of Kansas went back and re-contacted close to 600 children whose television watching as preschoolers they had tracked back in the 1980s. The kids were now all in high school, and the researchers found—to their astonishment—that the kids who had watched Sesame Street the most as four and five-year olds were still doing better in school than those who didn't.[6]

Sesame Street was the first large-scale experiment with using media for learning. It allowed program designers to tailor instruction so that it is meaningful, relevant and developmentally appropriate for its audience. Today it is possible to take the success of *Sesame Street* a step further to develop effective media-based instruction for older student audiences. These programs can become a union of work and play.

CREATING A KNOWLEDGE BASE

Most psychologists agree that an extensive knowledge base is required before students can do even the most fundamental academic skills such as reading and writing. This means that if they cannot locate the appropriate knowledge structure related to what they are learning, they won't be able to understand it.[7]

A student who doesn't know anything about the Civil War would not be able to comprehend text about the Civil War even if he or she were a highly competent reader.

Knowledge is required in order to speak, read, and write adequately, but these abilities are also the tools required to gain the knowledge in the first place. This creates a real problem in that—how can it be possible to increase a student's knowledge base when they do not have the verbal skills in order to do so?

Presenting some basic content through media can help students gain knowledge in a nonverbal format. This may be especially important for English-language learners and lower achievers. One educational technology company, *Discovery Education*, is already having success in this area:

> [Activities] include audio, animation, video and images, all of which are intended to make the material engaging and comprehensible to diverse learners. Students watch an interactive video on the layers of the earth. While watching the video, they dragged words to parts of a model of the earth and labeled its layers. Another activity involves creating their own ecosystem; students dragged different components, such as parks, ponds or parking lots into a wildlife area, and then checked repeatedly to see how changes in their design affected the survival of wildlife in the area.[8]

Having been exposed to knowledge through a visual and auditory method, it can help students to become more ready for the content. Even when new information cannot be conveyed directly through media, there can be opportunities to supplement the information with video, games, and even virtual reality. These experiences can help cement the knowledge and make it more permanent. Students greatly enjoy these kinds of experiences and will attend to them at a higher degree.

According to a book about the potential for virtual reality in learning:

> When English language learners have access to immersive technology, they are no longer hindered by understanding, because the experience speaks for itself. Companies are beginning to create tools that use the benefits of immersive technology to support communication. Students can experience learning no matter their level of language proficiency, and they can build on the needed vocabulary without losing the opportunity for knowledge acquisition in the process.[9]

It is a way to modify the classroom to become an active sensory environment for learning and can greatly enhance the learning process, especially for those learners who have not been engaged or successful in traditional ways.

LEARNING THROUGH MODELING

It has been long known that learning can occur by observing and imitating others, and this is called *modeling*. Albert Bandura (1925–present), a behavior psychologist, conducted famous experiments on modeling. In his studies, an adult researcher punches and kicks a Bobo Doll while a child watches. Predicatively, children who viewed the punching and kicking of the Bobo Doll also punched and kicked the Bobo Doll. Bandura created a social learning theory to explain that people can learn something just by watching or observing it.[10]

Bandura studied the negative effects of modeling, and much has been made of the subject of negative viewing behaviors. Violence on television and in video games has been long blamed for corrupting the behavior of youths. Violent movies and video games are produced in abundance in our society, but there has been a comprehensive lack of positive cases of modeling. Instructional techniques, for the most part, have ignored the process of modeling on learning.

Students will pay attention to models that they hold in some respect. For young children, this usually means parents, older siblings, and teachers. For teenagers, it can be their friends, Internet personalities, or movie stars. Modeling often has little to do with the specific actions of the model. If models are attractive, popular, or successful, students will imitate them for those reasons alone.

When instructing older learners, having a successful model explain key points of a learning situation can heighten attention and motivation, even if the model only acts as a high-level host. This may be enough for them to stay on track with learning even if the subject matter is somewhat dull. When Tiger Woods explains the principles of golf, learners take notice.

Modeling can also be particularly successful in teaching physical skills because in many cases, these skills have to be witnessed and cannot be explained well verbally. Currently, millions of people learn all kinds of skills from watching instructional videos on YouTube and other sites. Students should also have opportunities to learn by viewing videos. After completion, they can use the skills learned for a project or activity.

EXPERIENCING POSITIVE CASES

When experiencing meaningful events in the world, it can lead to greater overall awareness. It is an unfortunate truth that many teenagers and adults can make poor judgments. Older learners need to be exposed to ways of cooperation, altruism, and respect for others. They will carry these learned behaviors with them throughout their lives.

> Whatever we practice repeatedly affects the brain. If we practice aggressive ways of thinking, feeling, and reacting, "then we will get better at those." While it's difficult to attribute causality, he said, when we "practice being vigilant for enemies and then reacting quickly to potentially aggressive threats, we are rehearsing this [pro-social] script."[11]

In children's stories and fairy tales, there is usually a battle between good and evil with good ultimately prevailing. This is a primary way that children learn "right" from "wrong" in a visual story format. Experiencing cases that differentiate good behavior from bad behavior should not end in childhood but should continue well into adulthood. For example, studies suggest that young people can show gains in civic knowledge and behavior from playing a commercial video game such as Civilization.

> Players begin in the Stone Age and move all the way to the twenty-first century. In the process, they make a wide range of decisions about when to introduce reading, religion, and the printing press. They negotiate trade agreements and at the same time are responsible for the day-to-day political and financial governance of the city. Through this simulation, participants have the opportunities to learn about the dynamics of economic, political, and legal systems.
>
> Engaging in this way provides opportunities for participants to develop civic identities as they see and experience themselves as civic leaders. Indeed, research in social psychology finds that such opportunities lead individuals "to adopt attitudes and cognitions consistent with the behaviors they are acting out." In addition, those engaging in the simulation have opportunities to practice and develop civic skills.[12]

Computers and media can infuse students directly in prosocial activities, allowing them to learn from their actions. Another way that positive experiences can input learning is through the *participatory culture*. A participatory culture has these characteristics: it must be interest driven, production centered, and openly networked.

> A participatory culture is a culture with relatively low barriers to artistic expression and civic engagement, strong support for creating and sharing one's creations, and some type of informal mentorship whereby what is known by the most experienced is passed along to novices. A participatory culture is also one in which members believe their contributions matter and feel some degree of social connection with one another (at the least they care what other people think about what they have created).[13]

Learners can produce a video based on an issue of their choice—gun control, for example. When the video is made available to others to view, the learner can feel the positive rewards that their prosocial actions are making on others. The important point is that the causes must be selected by the learner, there must be a tangible product that is produced by the effort, and it must be available for others to see—at least to those that are also interested in that same cause.

When these sorts of activities are provided to students, they can experience intense motivation and rewards for their efforts. They can also dig deeply into the related content, and learn at a higher degree, as the success of their effort requires that they present a compelling case. Leveraging the power of social causes can help learners process knowledge deeply and promote strong civic awareness.

LEARNING IN THE AFFECTIVE DOMAIN

Learning with respect to promoting certain attitudes is referred to as learning within the affective domain. But attitudes generally do not direct behavior; instead attitudes affect *motivation*. Educational technology has a great potential to expand affective learning when it has been typically difficult to do so in other ways. Directly experiencing something can allow a learner to "feel" the rewarding results and cause them to develop a positive attitude toward it. Actually experiencing events or vocations will make these activities more desirable.

It has been increasingly noted that many young adults are having difficulties determining a direction in life. They have often been accused of having "no motivation to succeed" or are a "failure to launch." There has even been an inability to attract people to apprenticeship programs. It seems like a no-brainer that someone would want to join a program that has a guaranteed $50,000–$80,000 a year job upon completion, but many people are still hesitant to complete the program. Most likely this is because they have never directly *experienced* the profession in a meaningful way. According to Leonard Sax in his book *Boys Adrift:*

> Four years as an apprentice, two years as a journeyman, then you take the exam. If you pass, you're a master plumber. And we explained this to every boy in the class. We said, just stick with this, just learn this trade, and you are literally set for life. What happened? After one month, more than half the boys had quit. They just had no interest in working. They just didn't care. Earning lots of money just seems to have no appeal to them.[14]

It is true that extrinsic rewards for learning can wane as students grow older, and this is why it is important to introduce intrinsic rewards into learning. If students are first exposed to the more engaging aspects of a profession, such as what a plumber does through a simulated bathroom renovation, for example, they could feel the intrinsic rewards. It is time to allow the private sector to contribute meaningful media-based learning experiences to schools so that students can directly experience those events and feel the positive rewards.

In prior generations, young adults went into the family business or trade within their community. They experienced these professions throughout their upbringing, so it was not foreign to them. They could feel comfortable and even excited about the job. Today's learners are not being exposed to professions in any meaningful way but are being asked to make career decisions based on arbitrary details. They may make poor choices only because they have a lack of experiences from which to make good judgments.

Most of all students need opportunities to experience different professions so they can see if it is a good fit for them—meshes well with their internal abilities and interests. Through simulations and media, learners can get a "feel" for different professions. When educational software is available from a larger base, including the private sector, learners can take a variety of applications. These applications can be woven into the related academic content and allow students to determine if they might enjoy doing it as a career.

Media-based applications and games on a computer can be every bit as realistic as real events. People can walk on the moon or explore the bottom of the ocean. Directly experiencing these events will allow students to feel the excitement every bit as much as if they were actually partaking in the activity.

Any subject matter or discipline can be organized and taught. However, with needed content areas growing in complexity, physically skill-based, or with moral implications, instructors may believe it is very difficult to teach those areas. Learning outcomes such as promoting appropriate social behavior are believed to be less teachable and are not emphasized as much. But academic instruction should be in proportion to what is required in the workforce and society.

Changing attitudes, behaviors, and making learning more desirable can be immediate outcome of using technology. In order to fully engage and motivate learners, media and computer-based learning must play a larger role in education in the future.

CHAPTER 4—KEY POINTS TO REMEMBER

- Communication began through primitive speaking and visuals. A complex written language gradually evolved, but there has been a return to simple communication including the use of images with the growth of globalization.
- Learning through visuals and media can help create a base of knowledge, from which more complex information may be assimilated. *Sesame Street* was one of the first cases of using media to learn and has been very successful in creating learning readiness in children. Media can take the next step to promote learning readiness for adolescents and adults.
- Much of learning occurs by viewing the actions of others. Models can teach in areas that have traditionally been difficult or dull. Students will have heightened attention to models that they admire.
- Experiencing prosocial cases can allow students to practice ethical behavior. Learning within the affective domain with the intent to alter attitudes can be the most lasting learning that students will have. It can allow them to get a "feel" for certain vocations and skills.

NOTES

1. Christian Van Der Velde, MD, *The Mind, Its Nature and Origin*. Amherst, NY: Prometheus Books, 2004 (p. 19).

2. E. W. Eisner, "The Celebration of Thinking." In K. M. Cauley, F. Linder, and J. H. McMillan (Eds.), *Annual Editions: Educational Psychology*, 90/01. Guilford, CT: Dushkin (p. 77).

3. Bernie Trilling and Charles Fadel, *21st Century Skills: Learning for Life in Our Times,* San Francisco, CA: Jossey-Bass, 2009 (p. 68).

4. M. A. White, "Images Foster Greater Learning," *Electronic Learning,* 11(1), 6, 1991.

5. Elysa Gardner, "At 40, Sesame Street Is in a Constant State of Renewal," *USA Today,* November 6, 2009.

6. Malcolm Gladwell, *The Tipping Point: How Little Things Can Make a Big Difference*. New York: Little, Brown and Company, 2002 (p. 285).

7. E. D. Hirsch, Jr., *The Knowledge Deficit: Closing the Shocking Education Gap for American Children*, New York: Houghton Mifflin, 2006 (p. 72).

8. Mark Warschauer, *Learning in the Cloud, How (and Why) to Transform Schools with Digital Media*. New York: Teachers College Press, 2011 (p. 42).

9. Jaime Donally, *Learning Transported—Augmented, Virtual and Mixed Reality for All Classrooms*, ISTE: ISBN 978-1-56484-33-9, 2018 (p. 11).

10. Adam Cash, *Psychology for Dummies: A Reference for the Rest of Us*. Indianapolis, IN: Wiley Publishing, Inc., 2002 (p. 142).

11. Greg Toppo, *The Game Believes in You—How Digital Play Can Make Our Kids Smarter*. New York: Palgrave Macmillan, 2015 (p. 201).

12. Joseph Kahne, Ellen Middaugh, and Chris Evans, *The Civic Potential of Video Games*. Cambridge, MA: The MIT Press, 2009 (pp. 17–18).

13. Carrie James, *Young People, Ethics, and the New Digital Media, a Synthesis from the Goodplay Project*. Cambridge: The MIP Press, 2009 (p. 7).

14. Leonard Sax, *Boys Adrift: The Five Factors Driving the Growing Epidemic of Unmotivated Boys and Underachieving Young Men*. Philadelphia. PA: Basic Books, 2007 (pp. 118–119).

Chapter 5

Improving Basic Skills

Human behavior is 100 percent under the control of the genes and 100 percent under the control of the environment.
—Nobel laureate Peter Medawar

This chapter explores the psychological theories of behaviorism, which had traditionally been central to the understanding of how procedural skills are developed. Behaviorist principles are not currently popular with schools, but there are many important insights that can be gained from these theories. By utilizing educational technology that is based on certain behaviorist principles, there can be ways to greatly enhance learning.

The psychological theories of behaviorism really came about from the ideas of Charles Darwin, and they are based on the idea that learning occurs because it is needed in the environment. Learning occurs because it is rewarding and adaptive in nature. The theories of behaviorism have always been highly provable scientifically. Rats can learn many tasks when they are presented with food as a reward.[1] However, making the proverbial leap from learning in animals to learning in people is, of course, not at all simple and straightforward. Yet efforts have been made to do just that, allowing for achieving many positive results.

THE RISE OF PROGRAMMED INSTRUCTION

It was the behaviorist B. F. Skinner who created a form of programmed instruction that consists of breaking learning content into small questions or problems, which require an immediate response from the student. Feedback in the form of an acknowledgment of right or wrong is granted immediately after each response for "reinforcement."

Initially, Skinner's form of programmed instruction could be delivered through workbooks or through rudimentary computers—called "teaching machines.[2]" Students would make responses to these segmented items until they have reached a certain level of proficiency. Some students would take longer than others, but all eventually would reach that level.

There have been whole academic curriculums created into a programmed instruction format with the intent that *all* students can reach a criterion level of achievement. The success of these curriculums has been mixed. Some educators have praised the approach for improving the knowledge and skills of all their students, especially those who are lower achieving, but most others have criticized the curriculums as dumbing down content to the simplest level.[3] They believe this "drill and kill" method can lead to an aversion to learning.

TEACHING IS AN ART AND A SCIENCE

Utilizing behaviorist methods have generally not been popular because, throughout history, teaching has always been considered more of an art than a science. While it may be possible to teach simple skills through behaviorist methods, most educators believe that this could never constitute real learning, and it could never promote the kind of deep and meaningful knowledge that only a teacher can provide. In fact, successful learning has generally been credited to the techniques of a good teacher. One book on computerized learning explains the role of teachers very clearly:

> Acting, posturing, dramatizing, shouting, and gesturing are styles an instructor may choose to add drama and excitement to what can easily become a boring process. Great instructors all have a style that works for them, and I doubt that it can be taught or even successfully imitated. It is their unique, creative approach to the difficult problem of persuading people to do what they are reluctant to do.[4]

Since teacher effectiveness is widely considered to be the most important element to a successful learning experience, educators have long been uncomfortable with the idea that human learning could be performed through scientific methods much like what is done with animals. However, as a supplement to traditional learning, behaviorist methods may be able to help in a number of important ways.

IMPROVING ACADEMIC SKILLS

When students are having trouble in a content area, computer-assisted instruction can provide a much-needed achievement boost. Programmed instruction can be provided to all learners so they can achieve at a higher level. This can especially be done in the needed areas of English language arts and math, where current educational standards require increased proficiency. As noted in the very popular book *Future Shock*:

> Computer-assisted education, programmed instruction, and other such techniques, despite popular misconceptions, radically enhance the possibility of diversity in the classroom. They permit each student to advance at his or her own purely personal pace. They permit each student to follow a custom-cut path toward knowledge.[5]

As most people are aware, it is not the poorest students who receive the most assistance through personalized tutoring. It is really the most economically privilaged students who in fact get the most tutoring, especially through their parents. Generally poorer students do not have access to consistent and high-quality tutoring. This is an unfortunate fact and one that can be overcome through the use of technology.

Supplemental tutorials and drill-and-practice, in the same way that flash cards have always been used, can also be provided so students can achieve at a higher level. There is one area where supplemental practice has been widely used with success. It is within the area of foreign language learning. Within typical classroom foreign language learning, there generally is not enough time or practice to develop language fluency.

Currently in most foreign language classes, learners do practice activities on their own. They view videos, where they can repeat phrases and answer questions. In the same way that foreign language development has been improved through supplemental practice, all academic areas could benefit from additional practice. And like foreign language learning, students can practice with these programs in a way that is nongraded and therefore nonstressful.

IMPROVING REAL-WORLD SKILLS

The primary focus of schools has always been to teach general academic skills. However, one prominent institution began to explore the idea that formal instruction could also begin to teach specific real-world skills—the U.S. Military. In fact, starting around the beginning of the World War II, the U.S. Military was facing a pretty significant problem. They needed to find a way to teach all of their soldiers to be highly skilled to fight in wars, and they needed to find a way to teach those skills very rapidly.[6] It simply would not be acceptable to send any soldier into the battlefield without the appropriate skills. The U.S. Military began to really look at the methods of behaviorism, so as to be able to design instruction based on specific skill development.

The ultimate result of these efforts by the military was the creation of an instructional design model. It is an andragogic (adult-learning) methodology by which content is written into specific objectives with practice and feedback provided to students during progression toward the objectives. The instructional design model was soon adopted by business and industry, and it has proved to be an effective way to ensure that *all* employees achieve the important learning outcomes that can contribute to the success of the organization.

In today's information-rich society, the importance for students to attain specific real-world skills, especially in technology and computers, is also becoming greater, if not becoming urgent. Similar to what the military faced, it should no longer be acceptable to send any learner into a complex global economy without the appropriate technological skills. It is now possible to bring the skill development methods used by the military and by business and industry to the secondary level and beyond. As noted in *Future Shock*,

> As recently as the 1950s, twenty percent of jobs in America were professional, twenty percent skilled and sixty percent unskilled. In the 1990s, the percentage of professional jobs is about the same, but skilled jobs have soared to 65%, while unskilled have fallen below twenty percent.[7]

As an example, consider how one learns to fly an airplane. Flight simulators have been around for some time, but they represent a new way of learning that people will increasingly begin to face throughout their lives. Learning how to fly an airplane may, in fact, be one of the first real examples of learning a real-world skill. These skills are often based on manipulating complex technologies—and when 30,000 feet in the air! Pilots practice with flight simulators so they can learn most flying skills to a level of automaticity. This frees them up to think in more complex ways when they are flying rather than dwelling on the simple mechanics of flying.

Students must have opportunities to practice real-world skills, including important technology skills, much like pilots spend time practicing with flight simulators. They need to begin to acquire technological competencies even before they enter the workforce. They can learn these skills through powerful simulations and even games.

LEARNING MUST BE "REWARDING"

Anyone who has memorized multiplication tables through flash cards knows that drilling works. But drilling doesn't always work; a central tenet of behaviorism is that there must be a *reward* for learning that acts as a motivator. Simply practicing skills over and over again will not work unless the learner knows that there will be an eventual reward.

It is interesting to consider that the same educators who attack behaviorism as "drill and kill" are putting their students through elaborate test prep courses where the students drill on vocabulary and isolated math skills needed for tests like the ACT and SAT. Many of these obscure English and math skills will never be used again by the students in their lifetimes, but this doesn't matter because there is a powerful reward present. The reward is scoring high on the tests, so the students can obtain admission to the colleges of their choice.

Of course, providing a reward is simple when there is a good grade or test score that a student desires; rewarding becomes a problem when rewards either are not known or when students do not desire them. For example, many students are low achievers and do not care about grades. The question becomes: how can learners receive sufficient rewards for learning when in most cases, the academic content is too far removed from what they are directly experiencing within their current lives?

When skill/practice methods are tied more directly to a learner's long-range goals and interests, this may be rewarding enough to overcome the somewhat regimental nature of these programs. Increasingly, students must understand the ultimate purpose for their learning. This is especially true for older students.

More Intrinsic Rewarding

If learning is based on rewards, something should be stated about the nature of rewards. There are two kinds of learning rewards as most everyone is aware—extrinsic versus intrinsic. It is extrinsic rewarding that is the most often used within school learning—and within the workplace. A student will receive a good grade for a certain amount of academic work learned while a worker will receive a positive performance review—and their paycheck—for completing their work duties.

Extrinsic rewarding can be very effective, but, as is well stated from abundant research, it is really not the best way to learn (or work), and, increasingly, it grows less effective the more it is used. The goal, of course, has always been to promote learning for intrinsic rewards. The problem is that it is difficult to specifically pinpoint what intrinsic rewarding really is. It has been loosely defined as a "love of learning" or a "satisfaction for work well done." To define it further than this becomes immensely more difficult because people seem to derive pleasure from all sorts of activities.

Some people enjoy the strategic challenge of playing chess or working crossword puzzles, while others enjoy the artistic expression of painting or writing poetry. There seems to be an infinite number of activities that people find rewarding, and what is rewarding to one person is not always as rewarding to another.

Because of the inherently unclear nature of intrinsic rewarding, it has long been considered as an internal or "cognitive" quality that is hard to really know. Yet one of the best definitions that I have ever run across on the nature of what is rewarding came from the behaviorist B. F. Skinner. He made the following statement when asked what he believes is "rewarding" to people:

> There are three levels. There are the values of natural selection: salt is good, sugar is good—now they're no longer good because we get too much of them. Then there's the personal: what is reinforcing to you, for your own reasons. And then there is the cultural: what is good for others, what culture reinforces for individuals because it is good for the culture and the survival of the culture not just what individual people like.[8]

When rewards are shown this way, it implies that they really reside on a continuum. The first level of rewards is extrinsic rewarding, and it is directing related to survival or primary needs. It is an interesting point because it can easily explain the unfortunate phenomenon that many people, throughout their lives, unknowingly strive largely for extrinsic rewards. Oftentimes they are not even happy about this—money doesn't buy happiness as they say. Only after their basic survival needs have been met can people begin to "feel" the intrinsic rewards.

Skinner's second level of rewards is for the personal—"what is reinforcing for you, for your own reasons." This is a very vague statement. If the goal of learning is to promote intrinsic rewards, how can this occur when what is rewarding cannot even be adequately determined? The answer, of course, is to provide control. When students are in control of some of their own learning, they can find what is rewarding to them.

As stated previously, most learners as they grow older will discover that they possess certain aptitudes—commonly called talents. When learners begin to partake in certain activities where they feel they have some talent, it can be rewarding to them. So, what is intrinsically rewarding to each person can vary and is most certainly affected by an individual's own genetic makeup of abilities.

At this point, it should be mentioned that abundant evidence exists that actually proves the exact opposite conclusion. People who have obtained amazing levels of talent in a particular area have done this through hard work, not through any special ability. They have spent hundreds and even thousands of hours of additional practice or study over their contemporaries. This implies that high achievement is really the result of hard work and not of any specific talent.

As noted in the book *Talent Is Overrated,* by Geoff Colvin, many people with exceptional talent, such as Mozart, did not demonstrate this talent when they first started out in their fields. Mozart's first compositions were, in fact, mostly plagiarized works of his father.[9] However, there is one important consideration in these studies that cannot be overlooked. It is that there must be some internal quality that makes people *want* to practice and study at such a grueling rate as opposed to others.

This propelling drive to achieve in a certain area and the feelings of intrinsic rewards that follow, I believe, occur when people find the right "fit" between their inborn abilities and a particular area of study or skill. Natural selection is, in fact, the process by which organisms strive to find the best fit for themselves in their surroundings. It implies that organisms will perform better if they can determine for themselves what is best for them.

But rarely do most people have the opportunity to find the best fit. Their path through the school years generally consists of a standardized curriculum. This most certainly should change; learners should have some control in the educational process, and this can most easily be done in the later grades. Learners should be able to try various applications of interest so as to be able to make the best choices. Computers and technology are ideal for providing a variety of learning activities.

The third level of rewards that Skinner mentioned was the cultural—"what is good for others and the survival of the culture." This implies that people will find knowledge or abilities rewarding that they see as beneficial or adaptive to their immediate social situation. Of course, these social situations can vary greatly as everyone is aware. What is perceived to be beneficial in a gang infested innercity neighborhood can be quite different than those perceived to be beneficial in an affluent suburb. What is socially rewarding most often starts out when people try to "conform" and do what others in their immediate social group are doing.

However, after individuals achieve a certain level of success with their work and life, a need for a social benefit can evolve into a desire to truly help others. Most people agree that the greatest satisfaction in life occurs when they "give back" to society. In this regard, students should have opportunities to work on applications and projects that are civic or prosocial in nature. They can, for example, pick issues or concerns within their immediate cultural environment in order to study and promote an awareness of them.

The three levels of a rewards also correspond well with a well-known psychological theory, that of Abraham Maslow's *hierarchy of needs*. In Maslow's hierarchy of needs, people must satisfy their basic survival needs first. Next, they move on to a need for belonging and security in their society. After they have achieved a level of success with themselves and within their society, they can achieve "self-actualization" which is a profound need to give back and benefit others.[10]

Maslow, in fact, distinguished between deficiency needs and growth needs (extrinsic vs. intrinsic rewards) in his hierarchy. The lowest four levels on his hierarchy he called deficiency needs; the highest three levels on his hierarchy he called gratification or growth needs. According to Maslow, learning for deficit needs tends to be extrinsically rewarding while learning for growth needs tends to be intrinsically rewarding.

Going from Extrinsic to Intrinsic Rewards

The learning style and associated rewards of adolescents and adults are different than they are for children. Children really do have a "love of learning," and they are motivated to get a general understanding of the world around them. It is primarily the role of the teacher or parent to shape a child's learning to what is most beneficial. The positive regards of a teacher or parent (extrinsic rewards) are very important for the success of young students.[11]

But as every parent knows, a problem arises when the students reach adolescence. At this point, the entire parental (and educator's) way of dealing with students seems to take a giant turn. Many young adults begin to show defiance and want more freedom in what they learn.

After the effects of extrinsic rewards of praise or grades begin to fade around adolescence, it will be primarily intrinsic rewards that will sustain learners. They will want to explore what has special interest to them, and their attention will be increasingly attracted to those areas. At this point, it is important for students to have some freedom in the learning process.

It may make sense to separate the rewarding system between younger and older students. Paying or praising (using extrinsic rewards) for learning can be extremely effective with younger students. Some pay-for-reading programs have been successful and have greatly increased the amount of reading with children.[12]

If extrinsic rewarding works for achievement, then by all means it should be done, especially for those who are economically disadvantaged. But extrinsic rewards lose their effectiveness over time. They may still work in the short run with older students, but they will not promote lifelong learning and achievement. Older students generally feel that they can be managed or manipulated by rewards, and that others can use rewards to gain an advantage over them.[13]

Unfortunately, for practical reasons alone, extrinsic rewarding will likely remain as the primary method of rewarding in schools and workplaces. If students are permitted to learn only what is of interest to them, then they may not achieve what is most important for work and life in society. Likewise, if employees are allowed to only learn and perform what is of interest to them, no company could ever get a marketable product out the door.

But intrinsic rewarding can go alongside the standard extrinsic rewarding in schools. Using some applications of the student's own choosing as well as those that are aligned their long-term goals may be intrinsically rewarding enough to sustain their efforts and increase long-term achievement.

When extrinsic rewarding is used too often, as is often the case today, it can make students pay too little attention to what is intrinsically rewarding. Some especially high-achieving students are learning only what is required for the test and generally are not expanding their thinking much beyond this.

THE CONTROL MUST BE WITH THE LEARNER

Abundant studies have shown that any attempt to control or impose restrictions on what is intrinsically rewarding greatly diminishes the rewarding effects. Studies of artists have concluded that when their work is commissioned, they report less satisfaction with their work, and their work is often judged as less interesting or creative.[14] Artists love to receive payment for their work but only when there are "no strings attached" and they are free to create as they want. Intrinsic rewarding requires complete freedom in the individual, and it likely results from the Darwinian prescription for organisms to personally strive to find the best fit for themselves in the environment.

Having students really enjoy what they are learning has never been a primary goal of formal education, but if education is going to be successful in an increasingly complex world, and especially for adolescent and adult learners, this need must be recognized. If students are not feeling any intrinsic rewards within a traditional classroom setting, additional techniques and some student control over learning should be utilized.

CHAPTER 5—KEY POINTS TO REMEMBER

- Behaviorism was the first attempt to bring a scientific approach to learning. Behaviorist methods have not been popular in schools because the methods are believed to be aversive to students, but this is changing.

- Programmed instruction can help lower achieving students get up to speed academically because it guarantees a successful result. Newer areas of real-world technology skills can also benefit from applications that promote extensive practice, such as the way that pilots learn to fly through a flight simulator.
- The way that children learn is more similar and is primarily motivated by extrinsic rewards. But extrinsic rewarding is not as effective with adolescents and adults. With growth and maturation, students will actually work harder and be more motivated from intrinsic rewards.
- Allowing students to have activities and projects according to what is intrinsically rewarding to them can promote lifelong learning. Putting any restrictions on what is intrinsically rewarding will tend to decrease the motivation, and so should be minimized by reducing grading processes that rank students against one another.

NOTES

1. B. F. Skinner, *About Behaviorism*. New York: Vintage Books, 1976.

2. B.F. Skinner, "Why We Need Teaching Machines," *Harvard Educational Review,* 31(4), 377, 398, 1961.

3. Ronald Smothers, "In a Poor District, Success with a New Curriculum," *The New York Times*, May 23, 1998.

4. F. Bennett, *Computers as Tutors: Solving the Crisis in Education,* Sarasota, FL: Faben, Inc., 1999, (p. 39).

5. Alvin Toffler, *Future Shock*. New York, NY: Bantam Book, 1970 (p. 275).

6. R. M. Gagne, *The Conditions of Learning*, 4th ed. New York: Holt, Winehart & Winston, 1985.

7. Richard J. Murhane, *Teaching the New Basic Skills: Principles for Educating Children to Thrive in a Changing Economy*. New York: Martin Kessler Books and The Free Press, 1996 (p. 7).

8. Alfie Kohn, *Punished by Rewards: The Trouble with Gold Stars, Incentive Plans, A's, Praise, and Other Bribes*. New York: Houghton Mifflin, 1999 (p. 287).

9. Geoff Colvin, *Talent is Overrated: What Really Separates World-Class Performers from Everybody Else*. London: Penguin Group, 2008.

10. A. H. Maslow, "A Theory of Human Motivation," *Psychological Review*, 50, 1943 (pp. 370–379).

11. Richard Lavoie, *The Motivation Breakthrough: 6 Secrets to Turning on the Tuned-Out Child,* New York: Simon & Schuster, 2007.

12. William D. Pflaum, *The Technology Fix: The Promise and Reality of Computes in Our Schools,* Alexandria, VA: Association for Supervision and Curriculum Development (ASCD), 2004.

13. L. K. Miller, "Avoiding the Counter-Control of Applied Behavior Analysis," *Journal of Applied Behavior Analysis* 24(4), 1991 (pp. 645–647).

14. Daniel H. Pink, *Drive: The Surprising Truth about What Motivates Us*. New York: Riverhead Books, 2009 (p. 45).

Chapter 6

Improving Higher-Order Skills

It's elementary my dear Watson!
—from Sherlock Holmes' mysteries

It is true that the range of skills needed for students to realize a successful future is larger than ever. So, it is important to explore how higher-order skills can be greatly improved with technology. In the modern world, the shear amount of knowledge is getting greater and greater, but the knowledge is becoming useless because people cannot effectively use or apply it. Their skills for manipulating knowledge are weak.

It was the philosopher and educational reformer John Dewey (1859–1952) who believed there was a "felt need" for people to think critically. As the principal member of the philosophy of pragmatism, Dewey believed that living consisted of an endless process of confronting situations that require decisive action.[1] Every act (including the decision not to act) represents a choice among alternatives.

Dewey held that if there were no problems to confront or questions to answer, then people probably will not learn. Solving problems and answering questions really comprise much of what we consider as critical thinking, and it means using either deductive or inductive reasoning.

IMPROVING DEDUCTIVE REASONING

Deductive reasoning is the determination of a solution to a problem. It is the process of knowing how to apply the correct strategies, and it is also the process of correctly applying logic to solving a problem. Pure logic statements (such as all As are Bs, All Bs are Cs; if D is an A, D must also be a C) have always been the most difficult for students. There has traditionally been a subsection on the ACT and SAT tests in logic, but students have notoriously performed so badly on this section that it is rarely used as an indicator of achievement anymore. Student's poor performance on logic questions is likely due to their total lack of practice with logical reasoning in general. A logician's approach is to take a set of statements that are true and deduce a conclusion that must also be true. For example, a common logic question is, "If all humans are mortal" and "Socrates is human" then "Socrates is mortal." This is one way to make certainty within the bodies of knowledge.

Logic plays a fundamental role in computer science and the upcoming field of artificial intelligence. According to Wikipedia, the whole theory of [computer] computation is based on concepts defined by logicians and mathematicians, including Alonzo Church, Alan Turing, and Allen Newell.[2,3] Alan Turing gave the first analysis of what can be called a mechanical procedure, and Allen Newell developed the first system that utilized the term *artificial intelligence*. Students need to have opportunities to practice how to "think" like a logician. From these skills, they can gain the confidence to learn computer programming and other technological processes, which are so much in demand today.

As a popular example, consider the Sherlock Holmes' mysteries. Sherlock Holmes could solve mysteries that baffled others because he had mastered the skill of deductive reasoning. He was able to successfully interpret clues in a way to deduce a probable occurrence. In one particularly famous Sherlock Holmes' mystery, *The Sign of Four,* there involved a murder where the victim was found in a room that was completely locked and bolted from the inside. It appeared that there was no possible way for a person to enter the room to commit the crime.

When Sherlock Holmes saw the crime scene, however, he determined that there was indeed a way into the room; it was through the chimney. But the chimney was too small for a person to enter. At this point, all of the other investigators were baffled because they could not even imagine how someone could get through the tiny chimney. But through Sherlock Holmes' powerful deductive reasoning, he determined that since the chimney was the only way into the room, the killer must be something "other" than a person.

Once Sherlock Holmes came to his deduction, he decided to look at nearby circuses because they generally have unusual people, small and what not. After he visited one circus, he met a man with a trained pigmy who the man had brought back from Africa. Through the regular clues, Sherlock Holmes was able to prove that the pigmy committed the murder.

Once students have opportunities to practice with pure logical reasoning, their minds will become open to the possibilities and rewards of using abstract thought. It was the early Greek philosophers who first noted that logic is innate, but learners must have opportunities to practice these skills in order to improve on them. Through exposure to deductive reasoning and logical reasoning required in many computerized applications, learners can gradually improve on their skills.

PRACTICING WITH ALGORITHMS

One way of allowing students to practice deductive reasoning is through applying algorithms. An algorithm is a procedure that will *always* solve a problem. Since algorithms are most often used in science, mathematics, and other analytic fields, having students practice applying the correct algorithm is a good way to introduce them to how science, technology, engineering and mathematics (STEM) fields work.

The emerging field of "data analytics" is the process of using algorithms to make predictions or applications in the real world. As one article stated, "as the amount of data used by businesses grow, there are new opportunities for analyzing it, which stands to change how we make day-to-day business decisions."[4]

Learners need activities and projects where they can apply algorithms to predict and prescribe answers for real-world events. For example, analyzing trucking routes via an algorithm can allow students to determine the most efficient way for freight to be carried on weekdays versus on the weekends. The complexity of the algorithms can be aided by the computation capabilities of computers. Students will then begin to understand the value of applying mathematical and technological interventions to the real world.

IMPROVING INDUCTIVE REASONING

Inductive reasoning involves asking a question about what causes a specific occurrence in the world. For example, after observing a magnet attract a nail, the question would become: what is the force that is causing that attraction? When an answer can be found through specific observations, the proposed question is often stated as a *hypothesis*. It is then the scientific method that is used to prove a hypothesis in order to determine the underlying causes that govern an event.[5]

Learners can gain a better understanding of how the scientific method is used in the real world by asking questions such as what causes global warming? Through project-based learning and data collection from the Internet, students can answer these real-world questions. Students are naturally inquisitive, so they can come up with questions about things they see or hear,

PRACTICING WITH HEURISTICS

and they can develop hypotheses about why things are the way they are. They can then determine whether their observations agree with or conflict with the predictions derived from their hypothesis.

PRACTICING WITH HEURISTICS

When questions that need to be answered cannot fit into a scientific method, applying a heuristic is often used instead. Applying a heuristic is a form of inductive reasoning, and it is based on pattern recognition. Heuristics are general strategies, "rules-of-thumb," and "best guesses" based on prior experiences. Heuristics do not guarantee an answer to a question, only a likely answer.

When people are confronted with a situation, they search their memories for a similar situation they have experienced before. For example, when confronting a malfunctioning machine, a technician would think about all similar devices he has worked with in the past, and then consider "would this same remedy work here?"

Looking for a similar pattern based on prior experiences has often led to breakthroughs as people try to apply their knowledge in new ways. The gold-crown measurement question from history is a prime example of how heuristics are applied. In the first century BC, King Hiero asked the philosopher Archimedes how he could find out how much gold was in his crown without having to melt the crown down. Archimedes was taking a bath when he recognized that his body lifted the water up in the tub. He saw a similar pattern (or analogy) that could be applied to the crown-measuring problem. The water that displaces an object when it is submerged could be used to determine its volume. This type of problem solving is often called *insightful*, since it suddenly comes to mind. Finding a unique or novel solution often happens as if a "light bulb" in the mind suddenly illuminates.

Brainstorming is one way to use heuristic reasoning in a classroom environment. When students can "throw out" whatever comes to their minds, it can lead to a process of finding out whether their random ideas can work. This is an important skill used in business to come to new directions and innovation. Brainstorming new ideas and innovation in general are often done through a process of *discovery*, and it requires that students can have opportunities for deep exploratory learning, so they can come to their own conclusions and "aha" moments.

Students can propose an inductive heuristic question such as, can smaller, more livable communities decrease global warming? Students need opportunities to use heuristics to come to answers not easily solved in the world.

Chapter 6

IMPROVING REFLECTIVE REASONING

Most philosophers throughout history believed that maximizing human intellectual growth and potential represented the very meaning of life. It was the earliest Greek philosophers who believed that God had bestowed special higher-order thinking abilities on humans. Socrates (470–399 BC) was particularly interested in the reasoning abilities of humans. However, Socrates didn't attempt to "teach" reasoning skills; rather he attacked the reasoning abilities of himself and others, forcing people to self-reflect on their methods for reasoning.

Socrates often presented reasoning problems to students. When they made mistakes, he asked them why they had chosen the answer they did. Through this questioning, students usually came to realize mistakes on their own. This teaching method was later named the "Socratic method." The Socratic method became a popular teaching method that is still very much in use today. It emphasizes the use of personal reflection to come to advanced understanding or to a correction to an error in thinking.[6]

It is crucially important to provide ways for students to reflect on their errors so as to learn from them. As mentioned in earlier chapters, the mind "defaults" to referring to its memories of experience when interpreting new events. This is called a "computational bias" and it involves the mind's preference for accessing memories based on their surface (visual) characteristics.

Examples of personal experience trumping over the correct laws and principles can be found in many places. For example, it is a well-known fact that gamblers bet money based on their experiences of winning instead of on the actual statistical odds. It is only after gamblers truly understand the principles of statistics that they can overcome these biases.

When people reach a certain level of expertise, they are able to access memories according to the underlying "conceptual" similarities instead of surface similarities. Based on their deep knowledge in a subject area, they can match novel situations to underlying conceptual rules and principles that are completely abstract in nature. Novices are usually not able to do this. Through extended and reflective practice, much like computers can provide, students can learn that their initial interpretations are inaccurate, and learn to apply the correct rules and principles, similar to what experts do.

It has long been known that many high-achieving students who can perform adequately on schoolwork and exams often perform poorly when encountering completely novel situations outside the classroom. Accomplished students often resort to their memories of experience (surface similarities) when facing real-life situations even when they have sufficient background knowledge from the classroom.

According to the book *The Unschooled Mind* by the Harvard psychologist Howard Gardner, there is strong evidence that reflective reasoning can be improved for advanced students through computerized applications. The following example is from the area of physics.

> In [the computer application] *Envisioning Machine*, the computer shows two windows. In the "object world" there are balls and a hand; the hand can grasp and carry a ball and also release it. The motion of the balls is like that in the world, except that the ball leaves a trace so that its activity over time can be studied. By contrast, the upper "Newtonian world" widow displays a set of objects that correspond to classical physics theory. The student has available a "pure" Newtonian world, which allows him to manipulate directly the properties of velocity and acceleration, a situation not practical in daily life.
>
> [Gardner concludes:] A fair amount of experimentation has been done with systems like the *Envisioning Machine* and *ThinkerTool* [another application]. Even when students are afforded ample opportunities to use these devices, some confusions and misconceptions remain. In general, however, students do become aware of certain mismatches between their own intuition and formal physics, and they make some progress toward mastering Newtonian principles and procedures. Used in conjunction with a well-taught course in physics, technological assessments reveal far better-informed students.[7]

It is immersive learning experiences that will allow students to act, receive immediate feedback, and then be able to reflect on their outcomes. But the point is that learners must actively participate in the process, so they can directly witness the contradiction to their initial understandings. Through self-reflection, learners can use their meta-cognitive skills to focus in on their responses and begin to self-determine that they were inaccurate.

In addition, many mathematical functions can be aided by computer visualizations, allowing students to really "see" the mathematical concepts.

> A mathematical relationship called a function is important in all kinds of mathematics. Algebra and calculus are really the study of different classes of functions. A lot of mathematics is very visual, and a lot of students are visual learners. But we haven't made much use of that in the past because obtaining that visualization has been a complex, tenacious and boring process due to the pencil-and-paper construction involved. Computers can make those computation instantly with display screens, built in graphics software, and they're fully programmable.[8]

Understanding higher math has long been a problem for students. Today's software can make this process easier and allow for the practice that advanced math students need. It can allow them to achieve a deep understanding for functions used in math and other STEM fields and allow them to apply them like experts do.

IMPROVING CRITICAL THINKING IN ALL AREAS

It is not only the pure academic areas of higher-order thinking that can be improved through technology. A surprisingly large number of subject areas today that fall under the category of career and technical education (CTE) require a large amount of critical thinking.

Within the automotive industry, for example, technicians are required to troubleshoot mechanical problems through computer diagnostics. Factory workers must operate and manage robotic assembly processes, increase efficiency, and decrease downtime. Even customer service representatives must assist customers by deciphering through a multitude of product data and parameters. As early as in the book *Megatrends*, John Nesbitt predicted the increasing need for complex "vocational" skills:

> The skills to maintain high-technology systems are becoming as important as the creative skills that design the systems. All across the country, buses, planes, utilities, even sewage treatment plants, miracles of modern science, are breaking down and proving unusable because we are unable to provide the companion miracle of modern maintenance.[9]

These types of real-world, critical-thinking skills can be simulated on a computer. After exposure to these types of skill-building applications, students can receive the confidence to pursue the content area even more—such as in a two-year degree and apprenticeship.

One example of a CTE profession requiring strong critical thinking skills was on the *Deep Water Horizon*. According to an article about the event, the standard training program used to train the oil rig's employees was not at all adequate for what occurred during the disaster:

> The paralysis [by the crew] was caused by the sheer complexity of the Horizon's defenses, and by the policies that explained when they were to be deployed. One emergency system alone was controlled by 30 buttons.
>
> The Horizon's owner, *Transocean*, the world's largest operator of offshore oil rigs, had provided the crew with a detailed handbook on how to respond to signs of a blowout. Yet its emergency protocols often urged rapid action while also warning against overreaction. Fred Bartlit, chief counsel for the presidential commission that is looking into the Horizon disaster, said Transocean's handbook was a "safety expert's dream," and yet after reading it cover to cover he struggled to answer a basic question: "How do you know it's bad enough to act fast?"[10]

Determining what action to perform by responding to multiple interacting variables in split-second time cannot be done by reading a manual; it requires strong critical thinking skills that have been automated from practice. Students need to be exposed to these situations, make decisions, and then see the results of their decisions. Only through a certain number of "failures" can they confidently act in a real situation.

Many high-tech companies, in fact, profess to their improving capabilities due to their uses of effective technologies. They rarely note that the success of these technologies depends greatly on the skills of the workers who manage and maintain them. These kinds of highly skilled jobs are the jobs of the future. Although they may not be academic in nature, they involve higher-order thinking. In many cases, they are highly paid jobs. According to the *Times* article, workers on the *Deep Water Horizon* had salaries in the $120 range. There is also further evidence that as students learn CTE skills, they can improve on their general academic skills.

> Traditional apprenticeship programs teach students the details of a specific job. The new programs use specific jobs to motivate a hidden agenda of mathematics, communication, and problem solving. Realistic problems at work or in class can provide opportunities for active learning, the "minds-on" process in which students can learn abstract ideas by doing things rather than sitting and taking notes.[11]

Real-world applications of advanced skill-building can help anyone learn the skills that are being utilized now in society. In the same way that a pilot learns to fly an airplane through a flight simulator, many other skills can be practiced in the same way. It would be beneficial for all students to have opportunities to learn within the CTE areas, even if they do not want to continue learning in those areas.

FEELING THE REWARDS OF CRITICAL THINKING

Critical thinking really involves using both deductive and inductive reasoning. For example, in the legal profession, a lawyer is trained to defend or prosecute human conflicts within the requirements of the law. Before cases are tried, lawyers must compare the case heuristically (inductively) against many previous cases. After sufficient matches are found, lawyers use algorithmic (deductive) methods to prove that the relating cases apply to the particular case to which they are working.[12] In this regard, critical thinking in the real-world often involves determining what will work in a given situation.

The process of focusing on a problem (or question) is powerfully rewarding in itself. Once older learners are engaged in situations that moderately challenges their ability, they can experience "flow" and their work can be extremely rewarding. According to one psychology book as related to flow:

> Creative adolescents and adults often achieved flow states while working in domains that match their interests and abilities. These flow states increase the likelihood that material within a domain will be mastered and insights will occur.[13]

It is important for students to have opportunities to perform higher-order thinking that is matched to their interests and abilities. As the world becomes more complex and technical, learning must become increasingly specialized. In order to compete in this kind of world, students will need to find their niche—what areas they can make the most impact. As stated in a book about the nature of collaboration work in the future:

> Collaboration is not group work where the goal is to divide and conquer. A common pitfall with group work is that one student does the lion's share of the work because he or she cares about the grade. True collaboration occurs when the whole is greater than the sum of the parts; a group can achieve what a single person cannot. So how can teachers foster collaboration in their classrooms, beyond their classrooms, and beyond school?[14]

Another way of using the contributions of different people with different talents is through crowdsourcing. As needs from all over the world increasingly require reaching out over the Internet to find people with specialized talent, students within formal education can play a part in this process. They will be and be strongly motivated in the process as well. Wikipedia is probably the best-known crowdsourcing project where people write Wiki pages to contribute their knowledge for the benefit of everyone. Creating Wiki pages represents one option to provide a crowdsourced activity by allowing students to write Wiki pages on content of their own interest.

Mozilla Firefox is another example of a crowdsourced venture. It is an open source and free Internet browser that that utilizes the contributions of many programmers to maintain and enhance. The browser code is developed through a modular approach, with each module being controlled by one volunteer "module owner." Any member of the public, who has programming skills, can submit a programming patch to Mozilla, which is subsequently advanced to the module owner. The patch is then reviewed by the module owner and designated peers to help determine its worthiness.

> What makes participation in the maintenance of a code module collaborative is a developer's sense of autonomy, in combination with a shared sense of mission. She is autonomous in that she writes code in response to her personal

experiences with the software. She is a collaborator because she submits her patch to a group of peers for review and possible implementation. And she is invited to choose what she wants to do.[15]

The Mozilla Firefox example shows how crowdsourcing is both autonomous and collaborative at the same time. An important characteristic is that students must be able to choose for themselves what part of the project they want to work on. High schools and colleges should begin to prepare students to meet this new form of collaborative activity. They can provide activities that are group oriented but allow each student to choose the portion of the project they would like to work with. It can allow the artists, writers, musicians, video enthusiasts, and other creative people to shine by allowing them to contribute what they love and do best for the betterment of the group.

MORE TARGETED LEARNING FOR ADULTS

There have been much focus throughout the years on how children learn, but there has been considerably less focus on how adults learn. This neglect is in direct contrast to the fact that adulthood is where people will spend most of their lives, and increasingly will need to do the most learning. There has been an even lesser focus on adolescent learning. The school experience for teenagers has generally been the same as it is for children, even though teenagers are much more similar to adults than they are to children.

When older learners can acquire new information according to their day-to-day events of life, their learning abilities improve. This means that personal interest and day-to-day situations should be contributing factor to the adolescent and adult learning environment. The adult educator Malcolm Knowles presented five assumptions about the adult as a learner:

> Adults both desire and enact a tendency toward self-directedness, although they may be dependent in certain situations.
>
> Adults have experiences and resources for learning. Adults learn more effectively through techniques such as discussion and problem solving. Adults are aware of learning needs generated by real-life tasks or problems.
>
> Adults are competency-based learners in that they wish to apply newly-acquired skills or knowledge to their immediate circumstances. Adults are "performance-centered" in their orientation to learning.
>
> Adults are more motivated to learn by internal factors, such as increased self-esteem, than by external rewards, like pay raises and promotions.[16]

For many underachieving teenagers, they are not obtaining any perceived success from their educational experiences because the learning is too removed from their outside experiences. They are not feeling the rewarding effects of achievement and this in turn is causing them to work even less hard on tasks—perpetuating a continuous downward cycle.

This is a way that technology can directly benefit the learning process. Positive and constructive feedback by a computer will always be consistently applied. Computers do not judge and are not critical. Computerized learning programs are vigorously tested and refined to ensure that everyone, including underachievers will achieve success.

Some people and especially parents may have a concern with introducing technology to a larger degree within formal education. Many parents have children that are already spending too much time on the computer or watching television. Schools may be the last place where students can learn and interact in the traditional ways of reading, writing, and arithmetic. However there is an equal perception that adults, especially professionals in the workplace, should be on top of any new technology. They should be able to grasp and utilize new tools as the come out. Adults should use technology for their work, while children should mostly carry out their learning with books, paper, and pencil.

Children interact with computers primarily for fun. They enjoy the gaming nature and expertly crafted media. In contrast to children, it is important for adults to interact with technology in order to gain important competencies necessary to deal with work and life. It is those with the strongest technology skills that will be able to use them to the most advantage in the workplace.

In short, the best allocation of resources for educational technology may be primarily at the high school and post–high school level. Concentrating technology resources only at the secondary level will also greatly decrease the expenditures required by the public school system, which is quickly entering a critical state. Not all students will go to a formal college or university, or will be successful there, so they need to begin to learn real-world skills while they are still in the public school system. In the twenty-first century, all students must achieve and perform critical thinking at a higher level than in the past, and educators must realize that it is not going to be possible to do this without some help. Educational technology can provide that help.

CHAPTER 6—KEY POINTS TO REMEMBER

- John Dewey believed there was a "felt need" to think critically and solve problems. Much of thinking critically consists of using deductive and inductive reasoning. Both can be enhanced with technology-based apps and projects.

- To improve deductive reasoning, students should have opportunities to practice using logic and algorithms to solve problems. These methods are important STEM skills in high demand today.
- To improve inductive reasoning, students should have opportunities to apply the scientific method and use heuristics to answer questions. They can conduct research on the Internet according to issues of their interests.
- Reflective reasoning is a very important component to critical thinking. It can be enhanced by apps that allow students to reflect on their reasoning, especially in the areas of mathematics and physics. It can also assist in improving skills in complex CTE areas such as what was required on the *Deep Water Horizon*.
- Using critical thinking is intrinsically rewarding to adolescents and adults and can lead to a flow state. Students can work on teams, choosing that part of the project which is most rewarding to them.

NOTES

1. Jhn Dewey, *How We Think,* Boston, MA: Health, 1910.
2. Wikipedia, on Logic and Deductive Reasoning.
3. Dennis K. Berman, "So What's Your Algorithm?" *The Wall Street Journal,* January 4, 2012.
4. John Naisbitt, *Megatrends: Ten New Directions Transforming our Lives*. New York: Warner Books, Inc., 1984 (p. 47).
5. Wikipedia, on Inductive Reasoning and the Scientific Method.
6. Derek Johnston, *A Brief History of Philosophy: From Socrates to Derrida*. New York: Continuum, 2006 (p. 1–26).
7. Howard Gardner, *The Unschooled Mind: How Children Think and How Schools Should Teach*, New York: Basic Book, 2004 (pp. 230–231).
8. Kenneth G. Wilson and Bennett Davis, *Redesigning Education—A Nobel Prize Winner Reveals What Must Be Done to Reform American Education*, New York: Teachers College Press, Columbia University (p. 19).
9. John Naisbitt, *Megatrends: Ten New Directions Transforming Our Lives*. New York, NY: Warner Books, 1989 (p. 47).
10. "Deepwater Horizon's Final Hours: Missed Signals, Indecision, Failed Defenses, Acts of Valor," *The New York Times*, December 26, 2010 (p. 26).
11. Richard J. Murhane, *Teaching the New Basic Skills: Principles for Educating Children to Thrive in a Changing Economy*. New York: Martin Kessler Books and The Free Press, 1996 (p. 122).
12. C. G. Morris, *How Lawyers Think*. Cambridge, MA: Harvard University Press, 1937.
13. Janel E. Davidson, *Insights about Insightful Problem Solving*. Cambridge, MA: Cambridge University Press, 2008 (p. 167).

14. Sharon "SAM" Sakai-Miller, *Innovation Age Learning—Empowering Students by Empowering Teachers*. Arlington, VA: ISTE, 2016 (p. 50).

15. David R. Booth, *Peer Participation and Software: What Mozilla Has to Teach Government*. Cambridge, MA: The MIT Press, 2010 (p.34).

16. M. S. Knowles, *Adult Development and Learning: A Handbook on Individual Growth and Competence in the Adult Years for Education and the Helping Professions*. San Francisco, CA: Jossey Bass, 1977.

Chapter 7

Enhancing Attention and Perception

He travels through life, constantly observing. He makes notes on all kinds of potential opportunities, which most people might not even notice. This is one of the reasons that he is so successful.
—A description of Mr. G.M. Rao, founder of GMR Infrastructure, a large infrastructure company in India. He is one of the world's greatest entrepreneurs.

People take in new information from the environment in extremely personal and situational ways. Because of this, student learning is often imprecise and inefficient, and retrieval can be partial and disorganized. There are many breakdowns during the perceptual process. This has always posed a real problem within formal education, because human perception is affected by so many variables. This chapter will explore how student perception and attention affects learning and how it can be greatly improved through computerized learning and technology.

IMPROVING PERCEPTION

Since the perceptual process is so complex, it has become popular to use a computer analogy for a greater understanding. In the same way that a computer can receive "data" in a number of ways, such as from a CD or from typing on a keyboard, people receive data in many ways. However, in the case of the human brain, it is bombarded with a large amount of visual, auditory, tactile, and other information nearly continuously.

Since students are inundated with more information than they can manage, they tend to focus on that portion that is the most meaningful and purposeful for their well-being. Meaningfulness refers to how well a student can "relate" to what they learn based on prior knowledge and experience, while purposeful learning is related to what will advance a student's own perceived purpose or place in the world. A large part of learning is really for practical or adaptive purposes. As one psychologist noted on the nature of perception:

> The basic need of humans is that great driving, striving force in each of us by which we are continuously seek to make ourselves ever more adequate to cope in life. Perception helps us to behave in ways that are likely to lead to this fundamental need for adequacy.[1]

It may be possible to direct the attention of younger students to vast and varied amounts of knowledge, but as students grow older, they will increasingly want to attend to new learning that meets their own particular needs.[2]

Determining purposeful learning is actually a key component to how training for adults is designed in the workplace. Before any training course is constructed, training designers conduct a needs analysis, which summarizes all of the work purposes to which the instruction will be directed.[3] The training design also tries to eliminate any information that, although it may be inherently interesting, has little practical value. This not only saves time and money in the design and delivery of the training, but also greatly improves its effectiveness. As students grow older, they will increasingly desire instruction that is aligned to meeting their own individual needs and goals.

Making learning purposeful is critically important in the working world, but it is critically important for high school and college students as well. High school students, in fact, are often heard uttering the following statement: "How will I use this information in life?" They are beginning to understand the importance of purposeful and real-world learning. This is certainly not a statement that someone would hear from a child. The mind of a child is designed to gain a broad and general understanding of the world.

I am easily reminded of a common joke we shared in college. It was "the definition of a nerd is someone who is interested in everything in the world except clothes." In other words, seeking to learn everything about everything begins to seem a little inappropriate as people grow older, but learning how to dress properly is definitely an important practical skill. Increasingly, as learners age, if they do not recognize a personal and practical benefit for new learning, their attention will be weak.

Finding effective ways to grab and hold a learner's attention is what dedicated teachers have attempted to do throughout time. They may set off a rocket to illustrate gravity or a use a flagpole to diagram geometry principles. These methods can fascinate younger learners, but as students grow older, they become less effective.

Older learners are continuously searching for more personal competence. This is the primary reason that "how-to" and "self-help" books, classes, and seminars are the most popular category of learning materials for adults. You are probably reading this book with the intention of gaining some knowledge to help you improve in your job. You may even be skimming over the parts that are not related to your particular area of interest. Adults desire to learn real-world competencies, and this need increases with age and mental maturity.

IMPROVING HOW INFORMATION IS PROCESSED

In regard to how new information is processed, another common computer similarity is between how the mind processes information in short-term memory and how a computer processes information in RAM (random access memory). When a user inputs data into the computer's RAM, it can be worked on for however long the computer is operating or turned on. Once the computer is turned off, all information in RAM is lost.

Short-term memory is similar to RAM because if information is not actively "worked on," it will be lost (i.e., once we stop thinking about a name or phone number, it will be forgotten). However, by rehearsing information—directly recycling the information over and over—the information can stay active in short-term memory. Rehearsal is certainly important for many day-to-day tasks. Consider the working day of a short-order cook. If the cook couldn't "forget" all those orders by the end of the day, the result could be a serious case of information overload.

Rote memorization is learning without a high level of understanding, and it is important for some learning. However, as most educators know, it is not really the best way to learn. Rote learning may be enough to get a student through an upcoming test, but it will not stand the test of time. "Cramming" is a time-honored study method, but permanent changes in brain anatomy rarely occur with rote learning. As one book on brain anatomy has stated, "when learning occurs in a short period of time of hours or days, the cellular changes will later reverse."[4]

Rehearsal stores information weakly and it produces a memory trace that is only loosely connected with the more established knowledge structures in the brain. It is really a process of meaningful encoding that is the best way to learn. The new information can then become "woven" into existing memory like additional threads in a cloth.

Generally, teachers use a "stick" approach to enhance perception by stating that presented material will be "on the test." They believe this will convince students of the personal importance of the content. The testing emphasis works well for younger and high-achieving students, but for most older students, it is not very effective. "Teaching to the test" will not encourage learners to put forth the mental effort to learn. For most adolescents and adults, learning to "regurgitate" facts is not motivating. But when learners can encode new information through the application of that new information to what is familiar and relevant, their learning will be more permanent.

Teachers and students themselves will need to identify key areas of content that can be reinforced through technology applications to aid in the encoding process. When learners partake in projects and activities, especially of their own choosing, it will better cement the knowledge and make it more permanent.

IMPROVING HOW INFORMATION IS STORED

There is a further computer similarity in the way that information is stored permanently within long-term memory and how it is stored within a computer's hard drive. However, unlike hard-drive storage, once information makes it to long-term memory, it still must be practiced on a regular basis. If there is a failure to review or practice the learning, it will gradually fade. The primary purpose of homework has been to provide practice of newly learned content. Homework is effective, but it is generally a one-time event, and there is a large variance on the degree of effort that students put into homework. As students grow older, paper and pencil homework assignments can lose their appeal and become less effective.

Learners require opportunities for practice well after the instructional process has occurred. The superior ability of experts, in fact, is frequently attributed to their use of *deliberate practice*. Deliberate practice has been defined as "highly repetitive, mentally demanding work that's often unpleasant, but undeniably effective."[5]

Experts use their skills of meta-cognition to determine very small and specific areas of their chosen profession that need the most improvement, and then they repeatedly practice those areas. When opportunities for practice and review are presented in a variety of learning activities, students can continue to enhance what is contained in their long-term memories.

The *spacing effect* is a learning principle, which states that when learning is spread out over a longer duration of time, learning tends to be more permanent.[9] Learning will be more effective if the material is spaced rather than massed and when taught in smaller sections instead of larger sections. Massed learning results in faster initial learning, but spaced learning is better for retention. One professor, Mark C. Taylor, author of the book *Crisis on Campus,* explained his success with smaller, spaced courses this way:

> Through my work with the *GEN* (*State University of New York* on-line course system) I came to understand that digital and networking technologies create different possibilities for organizing knowledge and structuring courses. As we attempted to market our classes, we discovered that some people did not want to take the whole semester, and that others wanted to combine elements of courses. In response to this demand, we broke some of our offerings into small units ranging from a single class to a week or an entire semester. People could take any part of a course that interested them, or that they felt they needed. We called this practice "unbundling courses."[6]

Specific spacing of instruction has never been a priority of formal education. Computerized learning can allow for distributed practice whereby information can be broken down through activities and projects and spaced over a larger period of time.

IMPROVING HOW INFORMATION IS MANAGED

In a similar way that a computer will lock up when too much demand has been placed on its processing power, there is a limit to how much information the human brain can process at one time. This limitation of human information processing was first noticed by the Scottish metaphysician Sir William Hamilton (1805–1865). He stated: "If you throw a handful of marbles on the floor, you will find it difficult to view at once more that six or seven at most without confusion."[7] With this remark, Hamilton became the first person to determine how much can be "worked on" in short-term memory.

Abundant research confirmed Hamilton's observation: Six or seven bits of information are close to the limit of what can be processed in short-term memory. But, when the information can be combined or organized, a larger amount can be processed at one time.

When information is combined or organized, it is often referred to as a chunk. A chunk is any information (phrase, idea, principle, etc.) that is known through prior experience. There are two ways that the chunking principle can be used to improve learning. One way is to break chunked information into smaller parts. Computer-assisted instruction is an ideal way by which complicated content can be broken into manageable chunks.

It is usually the lower achievers who will benefit the most from information that is provided in small chunks. If their learning consists of smaller chunks of information, such as what tutorial-style learning does when it breaks content into smaller units with practice and feedback included, the student's short-term memories will not become overloaded and they will be able to better handle the work.

Another way to benefit from the chunking principle is by learning certain knowledge or skills to a proficient level, such as basic arithmetic and grammar. It is then possible to free up short-term memory so the concentration can be focused on more complex tasks. This usually means providing abundant drill and practice activities on basic knowledge and skills so that they are learned at such a high level that they do not require any processing in short-term memory.

It has been shown, in fact, that many great acts of achievement are, in fact, due to the ability to effectively chunk information, which is based on prior knowledge and experience rather than on any exceptional talent.[8] Expert chess players, for example, are able to hold entire chessboard configurations in their head as one chunk and then compare them mentally to other whole chessboard configurations. Due to their prior knowledge of strategy, they are able to group pieces by the underlying offensive or defensive purposes in order to remember them as groups.

As a student's level of basic knowledge improves, they are able to grasp and retain greater amounts of more complicated information. There should be frequent opportunities for students to practice with basic facts and skills, such as what drill-and-practice programs can provide, so that students can gain basic proficiency in needed skills.

IMPROVING META-COGNITION AND MOTIVATION

As noted earlier, it is really the degree to which someone perceives the importance of incoming information (a motivational component) that will affect the conscious effort they use to encode the material (a meta-cognitive component).

In relation to education, it is not difficult to recognize these important factors in student success. Some students move easily through school to receive good grades and high achievement, while many other students struggle year after year and become increasingly lower achievers.

The lowest achievers have always been considered to be the unfortunate victims of their circumstances; they are that way because of their family background, their communities, and their lack of opportunities. The highest achievers are usually accounted for in similar terms; they are lucky in their family characteristics and learning opportunities.

However, there have been many noted exceptions to this conventional wisdom. Some lower-achieving students have gone on to do remarkable things in life. Success in school and life in general seems to have other factors involved. These additional factors can best be described as the ability to control one's learning, and the will or desire to learn—or *meta-cognition* and *motivation*.

BETTER META-COGNITION FOR BETTER LEARNING

Meta-cognition is the ability for a student to "think about" his or her learning in order to improve on it. The ability to consciously control learning is a distinctly human trait; learning in animals is mostly reflexive. Having students directly control their learning seems like an obvious goal but improving meta-cognition has not usually been emphasized within formal education.

Having good meta-cognitive abilities requires some age and intellectual maturation because these abilities are assumed to be housed in the prefrontal cortex of the brain, and the prefrontal cortex is the last part of the brain to fully develop. As stated in one book on brain development, "Major growth of the prefrontal cortex occurs at about the same time the youngster starts to think about driving the family car. This is the executive center."[9]

The function of the prefrontal cortex is to be the command and control center for the brain. It allows for integration and control of all of the other "lower" components of the brain. The ability of adolescents and adults to control their own thinking makes them want to control all aspects of their lives, and this very much includes their learning.

Adolescents and adults would certainly benefit from more control in their learning. Meta-cognitive learning is also especially important as students grow older because secondary and postsecondary school learning are considerably more complex than younger school learning and require greater effort for success.

IMPROVING STUDY SKILLS

One area of having good meta-cognitive abilities is knowing how to study in productive ways. It has long been known that the highest achievers are the students who have good study skills, which results in learning that is accurate and permanent. Some educators have noted that teaching study skills may be the single most valuable contribution of teachers and schools to the total personal and educational development of young people.[10]

However, schools have generally not focused on improving study skills within their curriculums. Instead students are supposed to acquire these abilities on their own. Students without good study skills learn more on a superficial level, and they often quickly forget what they learned. The students with poorer study skills can also easily become overwhelmed by assignments and give a weaker effort. There are many computerized study skills programs that people can take to improve their study skills within school or outside of school.

Time management is one increasingly important attribute of good study skills. Determining how much time it takes to complete longer tasks or projects is important because many students have difficulty following through on long-term assignments. Overcoming procrastination is a problem, especially for adolescents and adults. Computerized time management programs can help students finally "get organized." Compiling timelines, final due dates, and subordinate dates are critically important for meeting long-range goals.

Many people have noted that most young people, especially boys, have problems managing their schoolwork.[11] In fact, a whole profession has arisen in the area of helping students prioritize, focus, and efficiently complete academic work. It is unfortunate that only economically privileged youth have the means to utilize these kinds of resources. It would be beneficial for all learners to receive guidance on study skills on a regular basis. They will increasingly need these skills in college and in the working world. Developing good study skills and the ability to independently manage work assignments is a necessary ingredient for long-term success.

PROMOTING SELF-DIRECTED LEARNING

Having strong meta-cognitive abilities is really the way that students will become life long learners. As students grow older, it is generally known that successful achievement becomes mostly the result of hard work and persistence and not of basic ability. It is the self-directed learner who works hardest on most learning tasks, and the most successful adults regularly seek out ways to improve their knowledge and skills.

Studies of experts in all subject areas show that they continue to learn throughout their lifetimes and routinely question their current level of expertise in order to move beyond it. In fact, studies of experts in many fields have shown a remarkable similarity in their path to achievement. When the experts reached adulthood, many had internalized the teaching techniques they had received when they were younger. This means that the experts continued to learn on their own even after the period of formal instruction ended.

The experts used a form of self-regulation, which is the process of critically examining their knowledge and skills much like a teacher would do. They were then able to identify "gaps" and to determine the ways themselves to reduce or eliminate the gaps, either by gaining additional knowledge or by repeatedly practicing a skill in need.[12] It was this continued self-regulation of learning that separated the experts from the other students.

Studies of the greatest expert performers also showed that they were able to move past simple automated skills to execute more complex ones. Tiger Woods can stop a golf swing in mid-stroke if he feels it is not going to be good one.[13] As people reach expertise, they are able to consciously monitor their automatic functions and actually change them for the better.

Computerized learning can provide the means by which anyone can use their meta-cognitive abilities to direct their learning and become lifelong learners. Since the prefrontal cortex—control center—is mostly operational by the time of the high school years, it is the perfect time to introduce students to self-directed learning. Schools must begin to realize that students will increasingly be in charge of their own learning. By allowing students to begin to self-direct some of their learning through projects and activities, it can be an effective launching pad for self-directed learning throughout life.

ENHANCING MOTIVATION—THE REAL MAKER OF ACHIEVEMENT

Animal learning is directed toward receiving specific rewards or avoiding punishments in the environment. But humans seem to have an additional drive that propels them to continually strive to be competent in dealing with the world. This general need to achieve and be useful is referred to as intrinsic motivation.

The book *Drive,* by Daniel H. Pink, examined in detail the process of intrinsic motivation. It cited the work of the psychologist Mihaly Csikszentmihalyi, formerly at the University of Chicago, who has studied intrinsic motivation throughout his career. Csikszentmihalyi determined that there are three necessary ingredients for intrinsic motivation. They are autonomy, mastery, and purpose.[14] Autonomy is the need for a person to feel they are in direct control of the work they are doing or learning, which, as noted earlier, is a primary component of meta-cognition. The other two ingredients required for intrinsic motivation are mastery and purpose, which will be considered next.

Promote Mastery to Improve Motivation

It has long been known that students learn best when information is moderately different from their current level of understanding. There seems to be an innate human drive to become better and better in general capabilities.

When the learning is too similar to what a student already knows, it will be considered boring rather than to cause interest. However, if the learning is too different from what a student knows, it will be avoided altogether because there is nothing from which to relate. The challenge has always been for learners to be exposed to moderately novel events, or blends of the familiar and the unfamiliar, which will create the most motivating interest and puzzlement.

The need for mastery is easy to understand when considering the popularity of video games. These individually prescribed learning events are designed to challenge people at just above their current level of ability. People can continue to practice their skills until they get better and better.

However, unfortunately, the need for mastery usually meets up against an equally powerful drive—that to avoid failure and embarrassment. As the psychologist Abraham Maslow had said, people learn according to an alternating need for growth versus a need for safety: "Growth is the result of a never-ending series of choice-points between the attractions and dangers of safety and those of growth."[15]

Evidence supports the fact that learning occurs best when it allows for mastery but also minimizes the risk of embarrassment or failure. Assessments that are overly results oriented—that is, success is determined only by how well someone performs in relation to others—are generally less motivating.[16] These activities, of course, include testing and grading. Activities that promote personal mastery are the most motivating and include projects or tasks that are ability-level appropriate such as video games.

The satisfying effects of personal mastery can be felt when the outcomes of student learning are provided only to them, usually in the form of regular informational feedback. Computers are ideal for providing this continuous feedback to promote mastery.

Promote Purpose to Improve Motivation

For young children, they are motivated to learn almost anything, but adolescents and adults are primarily motivated to learn something when they expect the result to have some purpose or value. As students grow older, they are less motivated to learn general knowledge and are more motivated to seek purposeful knowledge. To the surprise of many educators, a pure "love of learning" seems to go away with older students, and they seem only to want to learn in order to receive a good grade—or not to learn at all.

It has long been known that human beings are equipped with a mysterious searching drive called *curiosity*. Curiosity begins right at birth and doesn't depend on food or drink or any other biological reward. Babies and young children play with objects for no other reason than the sheer joy of manipulation. But as children grow older, as most people know, the curiosity drive begins to wane. Or does it? Everyone speaks of the need to "re-awaken" childlike curiosity, but nobody has really figured out how to do that.

Most likely, as human learning changes from fluid (general) to crystallized (specific) curiosity just narrows, and it narrows into purpose. As people grow older, the joy of learning everything about the world develops into a joy of learning what is purposeful and adaptive in the world. It is a means by which adults acquire the necessary knowledge and skills to be competent and independent. The fact that older students need to understand a purpose for their learning can be a real problem, since most academic knowledge is too general to have any real-world significance to them.

This can create a real motivational problem, and it is the reason why there needs to be some real-world applications of learning for older learners. Bringing real-world learning into the classroom is not always possible. Bringing real-world events through computer applications is readily possible. For adolescents and adults, they need to practice with their knowledge and skills in real-world scenarios.

If there is one principle with universal acceptance, it is that motivation leads to learning and, that without motivation, learning will be minimal or not at all. But even with motivation, students may not be able to reach their achievement goals because they have poor ability. They require good meta-cognitive skills as well.

As students move increasingly through the high grades and beyond, it is motivation, hard work, and good study skills that are the major factors in achievement. When learners are strongly motivated, they can study knowledge to the deepest level, and they can practice skills to greater levels of proficiency. But it is also very much meta-cognitive abilities that are required to allow learners to self-regulate and direct their own learning. Computerized learning should be utilized with adolescent and adult learners to promote the needed motivation and meta-cognition.

CHAPTER 7 – KEY POINTS TO REMEMBER

- New information can be semi-permanently learned through rote-memorization, but this is not the best way to learn. Elaborative rehearsal is the process of making learning meaningful, which can be aided by distributed practice and projects.
- The chunking method is a good way to learn larger and more complicated amounts of information. Chucking can be done by breaking information into smaller chucks, or by learning simple skills to proficiency, freeing the brain for other learning. Both ways can be aided by technology.
- Increasing meta-cognitive abilities can improve general achievement through the development of better study skills. It can also promote life-long learning when students become self-directed learners.

- Older students will be motivated to learn when new events are moderately different from what they know, and also when they understand the real-world purposes for what they are learning.

NOTES

1. R. J. Sternberg, "The Future of Intelligence Testing." *Educational Measurement: Issues and Practice,* 5(5), 1986 (pp. 86–93).
2. David Z. Hambrick and Randall W. Engle, "The Role of Working Memory in Problem Solving," *The Psychology of Problem Solving*. Cambridge: Cambridge University Press, 2008.
3. W. Dick and L. Carey, *The Systematic Design of Instruction,* 2nd ed. Glenview, IL: Scott, Foresman, 1985.
4. J. Howard Pierce, *The Owner's Manual for the Brain*. Austin, TX: Bard Press, 2000 (p. 531).
5. Geoff Colvin, *Talent Is Overrated: What Really Separates World-Class Performers from Everybody Else*. London: Penguin Group, 2008 (pp. 84–104).
6. Mark C. Taylor, *Crisis on Campus: A Bold Plan for Reforming Our Colleges and Universities,* New York: Alfred A. Knopf, A division of Random House, 2010 (p. 124).
7. G. A. Miller, "Information and Memory," *Scientific American,* 195(2), 1956 (pp. 42–46).
8. Geoff Colvin, *Talent Is Overrated: What Really Separates World-Class Performers from Everybody Else*. London: Penguin Group, 2008.
9. Jane M. Healy, *Your Child's Growing Mind: Brain Development and Learning from Birth to Adolescence*. New York: Broadway Book, 2004 (p. 47).
10. J. D. Novak and D. B. Gowin, *Learning How to Learn*. Cambridge: Cambridge University Press (1984).
11. S. J. Derry, "Putting Learning Strategies to Work," *Educational Leadership*, 46(4), 1989 (pp. 4–10).
12. K. Anders Ericsson, "The Acquisition of Expert Performance as Problem Solving: Construction and Modification of Mediating Mechanisms through Deliberate Practice," *The Psychology of Problem Solving*. Cambridge: Cambridge University Press, 2008 (p. 75).
13. Geoff Colvin, *Talent Is Overrated: What Really Separates World-Class Performers from Everybody Else*. London: Penguin, 2008.
14. Daniel H. Pink, *Drive: The Surprising Truth about What Motivates Us*. New York: Riverhead Books, 2009.
15. A. H. Maslow, *Toward a Psychology of "Being,"* 2nd ed. Princeton, NJ: Van Nostrand, 1968 (p. 47).
16. Alfie Kohn, *Punished by Rewards: The Trouble with Gold Stars, Incentive Plans, A's, Praise and Other Bribes*. New York: Houghton Mifflin, 1999 (p. 159).

Chapter 8

Promoting Better Memory and Assessment

Work is play and play is work.
—A common expression of people who love their work so much they become "work-aholics."

Achievement is defined in the dictionary as "something that has been accomplished successfully." Yet achievement in most educational settings is solely the result of receiving a good test score or grade; it is rarely assessed through the accomplishment of some real-world task. For older learners especially, there should be other ways to assess learning than tests and grades.

The way that students incorporate new knowledge greatly changes with age. Young children are generally *recipients* of knowledge; they are content to learn in a verbatim fashion and then to apply the learning in a direct way. As students enter adulthood, however, they increasingly want to be *producers* of knowledge; they desire to use new learning to accomplish some real-world task or result. Technology applications in learning can provide the means to help meet this adult need for productivity and usefulness. In addition, as learners grow older, their ability to memorize factual information can become more difficult and be much less appealing. As a book on learning stated:

> For later schooling—marshaled in the superb research of John Bishop of Cornell—shows that in the last two years of high school and later on, the balance of utility [against factual learning] shifts in favor of deeper and more narrowly specialized training as the best education for the modern world.[1]

By utilizing educational technology, educators can find ways to reduce the difficulty and disinterest in factual learning and memorization, as well as introduce new ways to assess learning.

MAKE LEARNING DISTINCTIVE

When information is presented in novel ways, memory is improved. For example, when being introduced to a group of people with the names of John, Sue, Mary, Bob, Juan, and Fred, Juan will be remembered, because it is distinctive.

Of course, advertisers have known this for years. One only has to view the commercials during the half-time of the Super Bowl to witness the effect that novelty has on the memory process. It is the day-to-day variety of learning methods (or lack of) that can really have an impact on memories. Presenting an older film may meet the needs for correct information, but the dated dress and mannerisms can be a turnoff and cause students to tune out on the content.

Technology applications in learning and visual media can help improve learner memories, especially for entirely new content. They can fascinate while they teach. It has become a standard within business training that varied modes of presentation, including the use of media, will keep the focus of adult learners. For the most part, trainers in the workplace avoid having their students sit through long lectures. As noted in one book on virtual reality:

> One of the applications of Voyager [a virtual reality viewer] is the hurricane Harvey experience that gives a full picture of the devastation that hit the southern portions of Texas with massive flooding in 2017. Through Voyager, students can become explorers with Lewis and Clark, Marco Polo, and Eric the Red. Students can follow the journeys of Charles Dickens and Ernest Hemingway. In addition to these historical explorations, the locations students can visit are almost endless.[2]

By simply viewing factual information in a new way, such as through 3D virtual reality, the information can "come to life" and be more appealing to learn or memorize. Providing distinction in learning can provide an exhilarating experience that lets learners jump in without fully understanding the facts. And, many of these virtual reality apps are available for free on the internet once you possess the viewers. They can introduce factual information in an exciting new way.

MAKE INFORMATION MEANINGFUL

Meaningfulness is another factor that can improve memory. Since meaningfulness refers to the ability of new learning to fit into prior learning, a person's interest and background should be included in the learning experience. For example, someone who understands baseball will remember a lot more details about a baseball game than someone who doesn't know a lot about baseball. Meaningfulness can be best described by the common 1970 fable *Fish Is Fish:*

> This story describes a fish who is keenly interested in learning about what happens on land, but the fish cannot explore land because it can only breathe in water. It befriends a tadpole who grows into a frog and eventually goes out onto the land. The frog returns to the pond a few weeks later and reports on what he has seen. The frog describes all kinds of things like birds, cows, and people. When the fish tries to make a mental representation of the descriptions he hears, each is a fish-like form that is slightly adapted to accommodate the frog's descriptions. People are imagined to be fish who walk on their tailfins. Birds are fish with wings, cows are fish with udders.[3]

This tale shows how people understand new knowledge based on their current knowledge. Since the intent of school learning is to teach students mostly new material, meaningfulness in learning is often overlooked. Meaningfulness is a key component of training design in the workplace. Training designers carefully examine the background, experience, and interest of those attending the training. But taking a student's background into consideration is usually not done in traditional classroom courses. Instead, instruction is directed at anyone who is enrolled.

For example, when I was a technical writer writing for a company that made industrial ink jet printers, I wrote two different kinds of manuals. The first manual, called the operator manual, was for the employees who ran the printers on a factory assembly line, and it contained the procedural instructions without a lot of technical details. The operators who used this manual would get very frustrated and annoyed by a lot of technical information. They wanted only to know the step-by-step directions for operating the printers.

In contrast, a second kind of manual that I produced was called the service manual, and it was written for the managers, technicians, and engineers who maintained and serviced the printers. This manual would contain information on every screw, bolt, and circuit in exhausting detail. What was meaningful to these employees who used the service manual were the engineering principles of the machine, and believe me, they got vehemently angry if any part of the instruction had been "dumbed down."

The solution to the problem of different types of students is actually to create different courses and/or activities and projects for the different groups of learners. Even though the courses cover mostly the same content, they are designed or presented in a way that is the most meaningful to a particular group of learners.

Most teachers do not have the time or resources to tailor their instruction to what will be the most meaningful for their students, but when there are supplemental technology projects and applications, students can find what is most meaningful to them.

USE MNEMONICS AND STORIES TO IMPROVE MEMORY

Memory for factual information becomes more difficult as learners grow older. This has always presented a problem in previous times in history as well as today. During these times, however, techniques were developed to overcome memory problems that can still be utilized today. In fact, in the centuries before the development of the printing press, memory was really the only means for communicating and transferring knowledge.

Fortune-tellers and mystics developed precise memories that were added by rhyme and meter. Politicians and public authorities relied on memory techniques to remember important data for formal presentations. It was only after the invention of the printing press that the importance of memory declined.

Mnemonics are memory strategies that have been around for a long time and utilize visuals, associations, and chunking to help people memorize information. One primary reason that mnemonics are so effective is their high reliance on visualization. Visualizing something is extremely helpful in memorization, and evidence suggests that the brain mostly "codes" information in a visual format.[4] There are three common types of mnemonics.

The *method of keyword* involves creating a visual that sounds similar to a word and its definition—good for learning a foreign language. For example, "Trigo" means "wheat" in Spanish. "Trigo" sounds like "tree." To remember "Trigo," a tree could be pictured that grows stocks of wheat instead of leaves.

The *method of places* uses a well-known location as the way to memorize items. To remember, a person can to walk down the street or through the woods to see the items to be remembered (such as viewing vocabulary items hanging off tree branches).

The *method of association* uses a chunking method by using either an acronym or a acrostic. An acronym is the combination of the first letters to spell a word: The word *HOMES* is spelled by using the first letter of each of the Great Lakes: Huron/Ontario/Michigan/Erie/Superior. Acrostic uses the combination of words to make a sentence. The order of planets from the sun can be remembered by this sentence: Men Very Easily Made Jugs Serve Useful New Purposes, for Mercury/Venus/Earth/Mars/Jupiter/ Saturn/Uranus/Neptune/Pluto.

With regard to computers and media, the sky is the limit in the ways that mnemonics can be used within drill-and-practice, media presentations, virtual reality, and even games. In fact, it is a well-known principle within psychology that putting factual data into a story format is one of the most effective ways to learn. The brain seems to be designed for remembering information according to a narrative, and it is most likely because episodic memories are the most powerful memories that we have. In very ancient times, the *myth* was the way that information was communicated to future generations. A myth is another word for a story.

One organization, for example, is leveraging the powerful effects of stories. The Harry Potter Alliance is a nonprofit organization, which uses the very popular Harry Potter book and movie series to introduce youth to civic action and deeper learning. The Harry Potter Alliance considers social problems in the world and then puts forth a simple question: What would Harry (and others in the Harry Potter series) do to alleviate these problems? By asking this question through a story character, it is a way for students to understand situations or problems through a familiar narrative that they truly enjoy.

The Harry Potter Alliance believes that "fantasy is not an escape from our world but an invitation to go deeper into it."[5] By developing scripts, narratives, and models, it is a way to introduce academic, cultural, and political concepts in a visual and story format.

PREVENTING FORGETTING

Memory is only as good as what is eventually remembered, and it is rarely permanent. The rings of a tree provide a record of the weather conditions in past years. The dirt on the soles of a person's shoes provides a record of where that person has been previously. These are permanent records, but memory is often less than permanent. Forgetting clearly occurs, and it's usually not the result of losing the information, but just being unable to find and retrieve the memory.

For the most part, educational settings have not emphasized remembering strategies. But adolescents and adults generally use a more practical remembering style that is most likely due to the adaptive needs that come with age.[6] We can witness the fact that adults desire "real-life" memory retrieval, because they spend large amounts of time reading magazines, newspapers, and watching podcasts. These events relate directly to what is known in real life.

In this regard, memories often improve when a student's knowledge structures grow through increased interaction with the world. Memories also improve when people become increasingly familiar with the facts, concepts, rules, and principles within a content area. As people reach a level of expertise, their memories can be so extensive and well organized that they can use them to interpret whole new events that may be very different from what they already know. This is called *knowledge transfer*, and it really is the goal of learning.

The ability of experts to successfully transfer their knowledge in new ways can be illustrated by considering an interesting example from history. A Swiss mathematician, named Leonhard Euler (1707–1783), greatly wanted to be accepted into a mathematics academy. In his times, royalty sponsored scholars through appointments to academies where they were free to study and grow in their fields.

Unfortunately for Euler, there were no mathematics appointments available when he wanted to go, but there was one available in the area of medicine. So driven was Euler to receive an appointment, he devoured medical books so he would qualify for the medical appointment. His intention was to quietly switch to the mathematics department at a later time. Euler received his medical appointment and proceeded to unexpectedly discover many applications of mathematics applied to the area of human anatomy. One such discovery was that the anatomical shape of the ear was perfectly aligned to the mathematical formula for sound waves.[7] This shows that as learners become increasingly knowledgeable in an area of interest, their memories will help them to achieve in new and unexpected ways—a key necessity for innovation.

Educational technology can greatly assist in reinforcing memory to the highest degree by providing the specific knowledge that learners need to advance in their chosen field of study. With the amount of knowledge exploding in the world today, learners must be able to selectively build on their memories so as to be able to use and transfer them in productive ways. This is especially true for older learners.

PUT LEARNING INTO CONTEXT

Traditional classroom learning generally teaches facts and principles in isolation, while workplaces have always required new learning to be applied to specific work tasks. This is a primary difference between pedagogic instructional methods and andragogic instructional methods. Oftentimes, forgetting occurs because there is an inability to call up the knowledge within a different context. Context refers to the "memory cues" that must be available to call up the appropriate memory. Like a large search engine software program, the brain produces a group of memories that are contextually related to that cue. The greater amount of contexts that are learned with new information, the more likely the information will be remembered.

Evidence supports the fact that context is very important to memory. In a classic experiment from the area of problem solving, researchers presented two problems to subjects that differed greatly in their contexts. In the first problem, subjects were asked how a tumor could be eradicated by a laser when the laser was too strong and would damage the surrounding tissue. The solution to this problem is for a number of smaller laser beams to be directed to the tumor from different angles. In the second problem, subjects were asked how a group of soldiers could attack a fort when, if they all came from the same direction, they would be detected. The solution to this problem is for smaller groups of soldiers to attack the fort from different angles.

Subjects who previously solved one of these two problems could not use its solution to solve the other problem, even though they had exactly the same solution. It was only after subjects were told that the solution of one problem could be used to solve the other problem that they were able to solve the other problem. Since the contexts of two problems were very different (medical versus military) subjects could not "call up" one solution and apply it to the other.[8]

Older learners will have an increasing difficulty remembering large amounts of information learned at one time and in one context. But older learners can benefit from supplemental computer-assisted instruction. The greater the amount of contexts, the greater the amount of memory cues. Older learners will then be more confident to recall what they have learned and apply it in the appropriate fashion.

Information that is learned in a vacuum is of no benefit to anyone. Knowledge and skills should always be associated with the contexts to which they will be used. Of course, this is how apprentice-style learning has occurred throughout the generations. In apprenticeships, skill practice is done within varying contexts (job sites).

In prior generations, learning for real life has always been different than academic learning. Usually, there had been an end to "schoolwork" at around age of fifteen or sixteen and then a beginning to contextually relevant "life's work." Learning for a career has always been done outside of school. In today's technological world, this is not a realistic scenario. It is imperative that students begin to learn real-life-related work before school has ended.

There should be a renewed interest in providing practical or CTE learning in high school, college, and beyond to make school learning more relevant. *All* students should take some personally relevant CTE learning. They can then decide if they want to stay in that area. Completing apprenticeships and internships can help meet the need for real-world learning and allow older learners to be exposed to new information as it is tied to real life.

IMPROVING TESTING

Within testing for education, there is usually multiple choice, true/false, fill-in-the-blank, and essay-style tests. These tests are mostly recall in nature, and they require learners to recall previously presented material. But older learners have a harder time and generally do not enjoy recalling prior learning in order to produce it for tests.

It is true that many adolescents and adults can really begin to dislike school. A large part of this dissatisfaction is because of classroom instruction's emphasis on mostly factual recall and testing. For many older learners, a real "test anxiety" can begin to set in. Young children usually believe that testing is a good way to track their achievement, but as students get older, they begin to question the usefulness of tests. They can often feel that tests are biased and do a poor job of assessing learning in general.

In addition, test scores can be used to compare students to one another—some of whom have been much more fortunate in their upbringing. Seeing this inability to compete with better advantaged students can easily let the underachievers "get off the hook" for failure. This creates a real problem for instructors when students continuously do poorly on exams. There need to be other ways to assess learning. By using educational technology applications, there can be ways to deemphasize the worst aspects of testing as well as provide new ways to assess learning.

One way to reduce the need for recall in testing is to provide *recognition*-style tests. Since these tests contain contextual cues, they are easier than recall tests. Generally, as learners grow older, they have a much harder time with recall. The graphic capabilities of computers make them ideal for recognition-type tests. These tests can include, for example, dragging and dropping names to pictures, pointing and clicking on specific areas (such as geographic regions), and/or moving and grouping objects (like steps or hierarchies).

Another way to reduce the emphasis on recall in testing is by familiarizing learners with the test questions at the beginning of a unit. Pretesting is a common feature of computerized instruction. When using applications that contain pretests, students can feel more confident since they will know what they are in for.

A final way to deemphasize the reliance on recall-type testing is to allow for *portfolio* work. When students complete projects, they can receive credit by adding their work to personalized e-portfolios, and these can later be presented to colleges or employers. This will allow for less reliance on ranking and grading and provide a way for all learners to complete projects at the level or style that is the most appropriate for them.

UTILIZE PERFORMANCE METHODS

Performance assessments have generally not been used within academic learning,[9] but they are often used within business and industry and within the

U.S. Military. Utilizing performance methods for older learners could make performance a new way to measure learning that is not based on traditional testing. Performance can be measured in a variety of ways: a score, a level, a task completed, etc. Computers are ideal for tabulating and recording performance outcomes. Norman Frederiksen, author of the 1981 book *The Real Test Bias,* explained the process by which he implemented a performance-based assessment in Navy Service Schools:

> On arrival, [Frederiksen] found that the best predictor of grades in a gunnery mate class was a reading comprehension test. He then noticed that teachers lectured based on manuals. He developed a performance test related to maintaining, adjusting, and repairing guns on a warship—a gunnery mate's real job. Teachers and students complained that the tests were too hard. But instructors started bringing in more guns and had students practice maintaining and replacing them.
>
> Mechanical aptitude and mechanical knowledge became the best predictor of success in the school. "You can change everything by changing the test: The real test bias has to do with the influence of tests on teaching and learning. Efficient tests [cheaper and easier to implement] tend to drive out less efficient tests, leaving many important abilities untested and untaught." The real test bias has to do with the influence of testing on teaching and learning.[9]

Learners can receive a badge, notation, or certificate for any specific skill achieved. (I can easily imagine a row of small badge icons displayed next to a row of letter grades on a grade sheet.) There don't only need to be letter grades on an assessment sheet, as one book on learning noted:

> Students and parents measure success through grades and scores on assessments. A variety and balance of assessments can reflect mastery learning, persistence, experimentation, and other innovation-age skills.[10]

Receiving additional certifications is something that successful tradesman have always done throughout time. They don't receive a grade for a class, as this would be inappropriate. Either they have learned a skill to a proficient level or they haven't. And making performance measures a new way to assess learning can provide a motivational boost to underachievers who are having difficulty in the classroom.

Performance-based assessments, in fact, may become the "testing" method of the future. We got a hint of this fact by viewing the popular movie *The Social Network,* which was released a few years ago. In one scene of this movie, Mark Zuckerberg is trying to hire a new employee for his company Facebook. But unlike a traditional interview, Zuckerberg brings together a group of computer programmers into one room to complete a task.

He states that whoever completes the task in the shortest amount of time will receive the job. We do not hear any mention of what schools these programmers attended, what courses they took, or what grades they received. The job selection process consisted only of who has the right skills to perform the task.

In the future it is not unrealistic to assume that employers in general will be moving their hiring process in a similar direction. Learners must ensure that they well skilled and continue to keep their skills up-to-date throughout their lives, as they will need to demonstrate these skills to employers in the future. There should be additional options for assessing learning, especially for older students.

CHAPTER 8—KEY POINTS TO REMEMBER

- Novelty positively affects the memory process as advertisers know and utilize. Meaningfulness is what students bring into a learning situation, in regard to background and interest. Technology applications can improve both novelty and meaningfulness.
- Mnemonics are memory enhancement techniques that utilize visualizations, associations, and chucking of unfamiliar information. Stories greatly improve memory and can be leveraged to promote deeper learning.
- Older learners have reduced recall ability but not reduced recognition ability. Using recognition-style applications and tests, including pretests and portfolio work, can help contradict older learner's reduced recall ability.
- Performance-based measures of skill development have not been utilized within formal education but could be implemented by awarding badges or certificates alongside traditional grades.

NOTES

1. E. D. Hirsh, *The Schools We Need: Why We Don't Have Them*. New York: Doubleday Dell Publishing Group, 1996 (pp. 157–158).

2. Jaime Donally, *Learning Transported—Augmented, Virtual and Mixed Reality for All Classrooms*. ISTE: 978-1-56484-3999-9 (p. 73).

3. *National Academy of Sciences, How People Learn: Brain, Mind, Experience, and School*, Washington, DC: National Academy Press, 2000 (pp. 10–11).

4. Christian Van Der Velde, *The Mind, Its Nature and Origin*. Amherst, NY: Prometheus Books, 2004 (p. 128).

5. The Harry Potter Alliance website.

6. C. Adams, "Styles of Narrative Processing: A Qualitative Shift from Adolescence to Mature Adulthood" (ERIC Document Reproduction Service No. ED 288 099), 1987.

7. Amir D. Aczel, *Femat's Last Theorem, Unlocking the Secret of an Ancient Mathematical Problem*. New York: Dell Publishing, 1996 (p. 45).

8. Keith E Stanovich, "The Fundamental Computational Bias of Human Cognition: Heuristics That Sometimes Impair Decision Making and Problem Solving," *The Psychology of Problem Solving*. Cambridge: Cambridge University Press, 2008 (p. 313).

9. Gerald W. Bracey, *Education Hell: Rhetoric vs. Reality*. Alexandria, VA: Educational Research Service, 2009 (p. 198).

10. Sharon "SAM" Sakai-Miller, *Innovation Age Learning—Empowering Students by Empowering Teachers*. Arlington, VA: ISTE, 2016 (p. 40).

Chapter 9

Applications for Skill-Building

> *A tourist in New York City asks a man on the street: "How do I get to Carnegie Hall?" The man replies: "Practice, practice, practice!"*
>
> —a joke

Teachers have always known the value of practice, but it can be argued that in today's increasingly complex and technological world, students need more practice of skills—a lot more. An important aspect to practice is the ability to reflect on one's responses, which greatly improves meta-cognition. Due to the interactivity of computers, immediate feedback is provided, which allows for this critical reflection on responses.

Having learners become more reflective in their learning has never been a primary concern in formal education, but it is crucial for long-term skill proficiency. Computerized applications for skill-building can provide new ways for learners to be more actively involved and meta-cognitive in their learning. There are many computerized applications for improving skill development including drill-and-practice, simulations, games, reflective "buggy" models, and artificial intelligence.

DRILL-AND-PRACTICE

The simplest and most commonly prescribed application for skill-building is drill-and-practice. The purpose of drill-and-practice is for students to learn basic skills to the point where it becomes a habit. The computer presents a question or problem, the student responds, and the computer provides feedback as to whether the response was correct or incorrect. It is similar to the way that multiplication tables can be mastered by using flashcards.

Utilizing these programs can ensure that all learners reach mastery—something not always possible within the typical classroom setting. Drill-and-practice software is relatively easy and cheap to produce and can greatly supplement coursework such as was explained previously in relation to foreign language learning.

Drilling activities are usually not the most enjoyable learning task, but when drilling work is directly related to a student's long-term goals for advancement, it will be enough to promote the needed motivation. There are also increased opportunities to make drilling activities more appealing through visuals, mnemonics, and stories.

Intrinsic rewarding can be achieved when learners are able to meet a level of mastery with the program. These programs can help underachievers have some level of success. Learning through drill-and-practice activities can be especially beneficial to those individuals who do not have the assistance of others who can help them, or for those who lack sufficient background knowledge.

Drill-and-practice can be further utilized for important STEM skills such as computer programming and robotics. Computer programming, like foreign-language learning, requires much time-on practice to master the components of the code. It can be difficult for teachers to instruct on coding principles because the majority of the time requires that students be activity creating the code, but many programs exist that can provide that practice.

> Students of all ages can write code using a number of applications. MIT Labs' Scratch (http://scratch.mit.edu) has been free of charge for many years, and students use it to create games, animations, and stories. Tynker (www.tynker.com) is a free-web-based app that teaches students to code at their own pace. Codecademy (wwwcodeacademy.com) offers free interactive courses on programming in Python, JavaScript, PHP, Ruby, and HTML.[1]

By utilizing these mostly free apps, students can work alone or together to complete computer programs or robotics and receive the required practice to achieve proficiency. A certificate or badge can be provided for achieving a certain level or degree of proficiency in the program.

SIMULATIONS

Computer simulations are programs that allow for practice of a skill set that is beyond the environment of the classroom. A well-known simulation is the wind tunnel, which is used extensively by the aeronautical industry. When pilots and astronauts practice their navigational skills in a wind tunnel, they can learn how to fly through turbulent weather without actually experiencing those events. As one book on computerized training stated:

> Simulations work well for subjects, in which the greatest challenge is not acquiring factual knowledge but applying knowledge, skills and beliefs in complex, unique situations. Simulations work well when the goal is to apply skills in real-life situations. The simulation provides a rapid form of interaction; the learner acts, and the simulation provides immediate feedback.[2]

Simulations are an ideal way to practice skills found in the real world, so they can help prepare learners for those highly skilled jobs. The intent of simulations is for someone to learn a skill to the point where failure is not an option.[3] Learners can practice with simulations until they have mastered a skill to a level where it is strongly automatized, and as if it were a habit. It is not difficult to understand the necessity of learning skills to the point where failure is no longer possible. Would anyone want to fly on an airplane when the pilot is not 100 percent proficient with navigation through a wind tunnel?

Achieving technological skill proficiency is becoming increasingly important as the world becomes more automated. Students need to begin acquiring these skills when they are still in high school. There can be an associated performance-level assessment such as a badge awarded after completion, so learners can show that they have mastered the necessary skills.

> Simulations consist of elements that represent objects or situations, and selectively create interactions to enable discovery, experimentation, role modeling, practice, and systems construction to be transferred to the real world. Simulations are reality-based games where learning results from the subject matter.[4]

As a supplement to formal education, simulations can play a powerful role. Students can be put into actual scenarios of real-world skills through simulations. This can allow them to get a "feel" for the skill and also promote a desire to continue to learn in that area. Students need opportunities to get a "feel" for different professions, and simulations, especially in the areas of CTE learning, are an ideal way to provide that feel. When simulations are provided to high schools from the private sector, it can allow students to experience these real-world skills. While it may be difficult for teachers to assess the learning from a simulation, a certificate or badge can be provided that is set apart on a grade sheet away from the typical classroom learning grade assessments. This may be one of the few ways to integrate real-world skill development in academic learning, and for *all* students.

In addition to technological and CTE learning, advanced academic skills can be greatly enhanced through simulations. As previously noted in the chapter on higher-order skill development, physics and mathematical principles can be modeled on a computer allowing learners to receive a better understanding than they would gain in the classroom. As one book on computer-based learning stated:

> Some scholars assert that simulations and computer-based models are the most powerful resources for the advancement and application of mathematics and science since the origins of mathematical modeling during the Renaissance. The move from a static model in an inert medium, like a drawing, to dynamic models in interactive media that provide visualization and analytic tools is profoundly changing the nature of inquiry in mathematics and science. Students can visualize alternative interpretations as they build models that can be rotated in ways that introduce different perspectives on the problems. These changes affect the kinds of phenomena that can be considered and the nature of argumentation and acceptable evidence.[5]

It is important for academically advanced students to have opportunities to learn deeply the important concepts in mathematics and science. They should have opportunities to reflect on their responses, so that they can determine where their initial understandings may be inaccurate and allow them to make changes to their thinking.

GAMES

Educators have long known the benefit of games. Putting somewhat dull material into a game format can increase motivation by introducing a competitive aspect to it. There are many well-known games that have been used for educational purposes such as Wheel of Fortune, Jeopardy!, Trivial Pursuit, and Monopoly. These kinds of computerized games can provide a more interesting way for learners to drill on basic skills, and be more engaging than learning through a typical drill-and-practice program.

For example, many schools today utilize review programs such as Quizlet or Kahoot to review factual information for tests. When students review these types of pretest questions, they can master the content and feel more confident in their ability to answer the questions on the test. Much academic content can easily be put into a game format, allowing students to compete against one another, which greatly adds interest and excitement to the learning of factual information.

In addition, with today's increased technology, many games have advanced to a larger array of uses than simply drill-and-practice. They have evolved to a level that is somewhat similar to a simulation. The primary intent of these games, however, is not only to provide practice of a skill to proficiency but instead, to promote motivation and exploratory learning through deep immersion into a content area. One of the first commercial video games to do this was the Oregon Trail, which was intended to teach about westward expansion in the United States.

> The Oregon Trail demanded that students consider how the parts of a system work together, how one decision affects another and how everything affects the whole. Developed originally as a board game by a twenty-one-year old history teacher named Don Rawitsch, the Oregon Trail became a primitive electronic game in the fall of 1971.[6]

Often called *serious* games, these activities are routed in some knowledge and can allow learners to get a greater "feel" for the skills associated with that area of study through deep exposure. As mentioned in the introductory chapter in relation to *America's* Army game, intrinsic motivation can be gained when students directly partake in a skill-demanding event.

In another commonly known serious game, SIM City, learners build a city infrastructure and they must weigh the pros and cons of the actions they take. SIM City is routed in the content area of urban planning, but it is not intended to teach everything about urban planning per se. Instead, students usually learn these broad principles through prior classroom learning.

SIM City is intended for learners to try different actions as related to urban planning and then to evaluate the results of those actions. If their actions lead to complete failure, then that is OK. They can gain important insights from the experience and try again. Serious games allow for exploring content in greater depth than usually can be done in a classroom. Learning in this manner can be intrinsically rewarding and highly memorable because students are actively involved in their experiences.

The psychologist Jerome Bruner (1915–present) has a very strong belief in the value of learning through *discovery*. He believes that learners should discover for themselves concepts, rules, and principles. Discovery learning is intended for people to learn in an exploratory manner, and also to insightfully reach their own conclusions. Learning through serious games can be enjoyable and educational at the same time. It is one way to lift the achievement level of all students.

> High-profile international comparisons show that our kids are falling behind others in places like Finland and Singapore in skills and knowledge. But in the long run, our kids care less about competing with Finland than about having schools that challenge them and engage their interest. A generation of teachers who learned division with math Blaster, history with The Oregon Train, and the principles of urban planning with SimCity now see games as just another tool, like a calculator.[7]

Video games may be one of the best ways to increase intrinsic motivation for learning, especially in the higher grades.

> Video games are the most efficient feedback machines we'll ever encounter. At their core, they're built around a constant stream of "mastery feedback." If video games have achieved anything, they've finally perfected the elusive reward schedule. In real life, we're rewarded [only] at the end of a task, if at all.[8]

Video games provide mastery learning at its very best.

REFLECTIVE "BUGGY" MODELS

Reflective "buggy models" have been around for some time. They originated from the term "debugging," which is the process of finding coding errors that will cause a computer to "crash." In reflective "buggy" models, it is errors in human thinking that are highlighted so learners can reflect on those errors.

In a Socratic fashion, learners can begin to focus on their own errors and actually learn from them. Reflective models can also provide tips and guidance so that students can understand how they can remedy the situation the next time. Reflecting on errors can be educational. These programs can offer a huge opportunity for students to work independently to solve programs, recognize their errors, and determine how to self-correct them.

For example, one program called ASSISTments allows high school students to reflect on their errors in mathematical reasoning. When the students enter their answers into the ASSISTments program, they are provided immediate feedback on their errors. They can also receive additional guidance through tutoring and tips. The ASSISTments program for mathematics works with homework problems:

> The traditional homework routine involves sending a set number of problems home with students; they do their best and come in the next day to see what they got wrong and to have questions answered. With ASSISTments, teachers select the problems for homework from the program, students get feedback in the form of correct responses and sometimes tutoring, and the teachers review and plan around the emailed reports they get in the morning before class.[9]

In addition to solving math problems, the ASSISTments program contains fields that allow for written responses. This is a way for students to begin to explain their mathematical reasoning, and it is important for teachers to know where the errors in thinking are occurring with their students. With most tasks, especially those that are complex in nature, errors are usually inevitable. Students can make a wrong answer even though most of their thinking on the task was accurate.

It is important to ensure that simple errors are not always held against students as this will lead to feelings of inadequacy. In many cases, learners are reluctant to ask questions in the classroom about their errors because of the fear of embarrassment. There are currently many schoolwork helping apps available for learners. When students can use these programs, they can feel more confidence that they can complete the work correctly.

Allowing learners to interact individually with a reflective buggy model will allow them to have diagnostic capability that is customized just for them. Formal education has always emphasized that learning should be "error-free," and that it is not possible to learn anything from mistakes, except to do "better the next time." Students are often evaluated on a score that is either right or wrong, but when students can make mistakes and then reflect on those errors in a non-threatening way, it can allow them to self-reflect and improve on their reasoning skills.

As most teachers have a curriculum already established, these types of schoolwork assisting apps may be one of the easiest to use and start with. Since they are designed to work alongside existing curriculum, they can provide a much-needed assistment boost to the teacher.

> Because teachers are those who design classroom innovations share a lack of funds, time, and frequently evaluation expertise, teachers using a new program typically receive little or no supervision, feedback or ongoing instruction after they've begun it. As a result, programs commonly fail—or, at least, don't show clear-cut success.[10]

These programs are an easy way to give assistance to students, especially those who lack help at home with their homework. It can help level the playing field when students are given immediate feedback and assistance on their homework and other classroom activities. Many of these programs are free of charge and available through universities or other foundations and were developed through grant funding.

Students need opportunities to work without the fear of failure. Reflective buggy models can give those students the confidence they need to proceed knowing that help is available when needed.

ARTIFICIAL INTELLIGENCE

Artificial intelligence (AI) programs generally fall into two categories and can be used for two purposes: knowledge development and skill development. In the first type of AI, called Expert Systems, deep knowledge can be provided to students allowing them to apply the knowledge to many skill-based tasks. Since it is generally agreed upon that expert knowledge takes up to ten years to accumulate, this knowledge when provided via a computer can bring anyone up to speed.

One well-known Expert System is IBM's Watson, named after IBM's founder Thomas J. Watson. The first major application for Watson was to be a computerized contestant on the *Jeopardy!* TV game show. And Watson was, in fact, successful in beating the best *Jeopardy!* contestants in February 2011. Now Watson is moving on to a larger array of functions in the areas of health care, government, customer support, and technical support.[11]

Watson won on *Jeopardy!* but not without making some "extremely wacky mistakes," and this is why people must still be involved in examining the responses by the expert systems. Expert systems can allow learners to practice with a large number of highly specialized bodies of knowledge, and they can provide motivation for continued study in those areas. It can allow anyone to play "expert" in a variety of subject areas.

The second type of AI program is that which is based on skill development. One very popular and well-known example of an AI skill-based program is computerized chess. These programs have been compiled according to how chess experts make moves that are superior to others. To chess buffs, a monumental moment occurred in 1997 when IBM supercomputer Deep Blue beat Russian grandmaster and former world champion Garry Kasparov:

> In 1997, Kasparov took on an even more powerful machine, a 1.4—ton IBM supercomputer called *Deep Blue,* in a six-game match that some dubbed "the brain's last stand." To the surprise of many, Deep Blue defeated Kasparov.[12]

AI programs can provide learners with real insights on complex tasks since they provide the best way for those tasks to be accomplished. They can also provide a strong motivation for someone to improve their skills from simple to complex.

One area where AI skill development programs have already shown strong success within academic learning is in student writing. When students practice their writing on AI writing programs, they are awarded "instant feedback on grammar, focus and meaning, organization, content and development, language use and style, and their overall writing proficiency."[13] Since this type of detailed analysis of writing proficiency can be a very time-consuming task for a teacher to perform, AI writing programs can provide students with a much greater opportunity to get "expert" advice on their writing.

Many students entering postsecondary education today are not proficient in their writing ability, and students greatly need more practice and "time on task" with their writing. These programs can give tips in a nonjudgmental way and can also be tailored to the exact writing ability of the learners, as the programs generally have levels ranging from the first grade all the way up to college.

COMPUTERS AND PEOPLE WORKING TOGETHER

It is true that in many ways computers can perform many higher-order "cognitive" skills more quickly and accurately than people can. They can apply a specific algorithm in lightning speed. People can also perform this kind of abstract thinking, but in most cases, it is not easy. It is these "hard" skills that are really the most recent acquisitions in an evolutionary sense. And, ironically, it is these areas that computers can handle the easiest.

Computers can best handle the kinds of abstract thinking required in subjects like mathematics and science. As the world becomes more complex and technical, people will increasingly rely on machines to perform many of those tasks. In this regard, work performance will increasingly consist of utilizing the help of computers and technology.

It has been the quest of modern education to put more and more "stuff" in student's heads, but increasingly, students will need to learn specialized knowledge in conjunction with their goals for the future, and they will rely on computers to help them manipulate this knowledge in specific real-world ways. In this regard, there must be a variety of programs to assist learners with whatever goals they may have.

In older times, students just dropped out of school when it no longer met their long-term needs. Now students must remain in school, and as the increasingly complex world demands that they learn more and more, modern educational settings have a responsibility to implement new ways to allow learners to target and self-direct their learning to those areas that are most beneficial for their adaptability and real-world success. Increasingly this will consist of choosing one area of study, and then learning the technological applications that are associated with that area of study.

Formal education must begin to introduce ways for students to control and practice their reasoning skills from simple to complex. The most highly successful people have a strong belief that persistence, combined with many different approaches, will eventually pay off. In that regard, they have a strong motivational drive for success. If one approach to a difficult situation doesn't lead to a solution, then they retreat, regroup, and try another tactic. One study called this a "grit factor," which is the highest predictor for achievement and success. "Researchers found that grittiness, rather than IQ or standardized test scores, is the most accurate predictor of college grades."[14]

It is true that within business and industry, individuals who got to the top of the success ladder and then experienced a precipitous slide into failure are usually regarded as a good bet to get on top again. They are perceived as winners. When Lee Iacocca was fired from the Ford Motor company, he was subsequently hired by the Chrysler Motor company and was able to transform that failing company into a highly profitable one. Confident people have an expectation that persistence is what transfers to the unforeseen situations that occur in real life. Skill-building applications must play a larger role in learning in the future.

CHAPTER 9—KEY POINTS TO REMEMBER

- Drill-and-practice programs can be provided to students so they can "over-learn" academic skills. These programs can be enhanced through visuals, mnemonics, and stories.
- Simulations can improve complex concept understanding such as in the areas of math and science. It can also allow for practice of real-world CTE skills and can qualify students to use those skills.
- Games can allow students to become deeply engaged in a subject area and to learn content through discovery, while also promoting motivation and team building.
- Buggy-reflective models are programs that allow student to reflect on their incorrect answers. AI consists of Expert systems which provide a means for anyone to "play expert" and other AI allows for practice of skills like chess at a high level.
- In the future, people and computers will increasingly be working together in order to understand and apply more complex information.

NOTES

1. Sharon "SAM" Salai-Miller, *Innovation-Age Learning—Empowering Students by Empowering Teachers* arlington. USA: ISTE, 2016 (p. 83).
2. William Horton *Designing Web-Based Training*. New York, NY: John Wiley & Sons, 2000 (p. 567).
3. Clark Aldrich, *Learning Online with Games, Simulations, and Virtual World: Strategies for Online Instruction*. San Francisco, CA: Jossey-Bass, 2009 (p. 53).
4. Sharon "SAM" Salai-Miller Virginia, *Innovation-Age Learning—Empowering Students by Empowering Teachers*, USA: ISTE, 2016 (p. 83).
5. National Academy of Sciences, *How People Learn: Brain, Mind, Experience, and School*. Washington, DC: National Academy Press, 2000 (p. 215).
6. Greg Toppo, *The Game Believes in You, How Digital Pay Can Make Our Kids Smarter*. New York: Palgrave Macmillan, 2015 (p. 100).

7. Greg Toppo, *The Game Believes in You, How Digital Pay Can Make Our Kids Smarter*. New York: Palgrave Macmillan, 2015 (p. 9).

8. Greg Toppo, *The Game Believes in You, How Digital Pay Can Make Our Kids Smarter*. New York: Palgrave Macmillan, 2015 (p. 51).

9. Chris Dede and John Richards, Editors, *Digital Teaching Platforms*. New York, NY: Teachers College Press, 2012 (p. 93).

10. Kenneth G. Wilson and Dennett Davis, *Redesigning Education—A Nobel Prize Winner Reveals What Must Be Done to Reform American Education*. New York: Teachers College Press, Columbia University, 1994.

11. Kit Dotson, "What Does IBM's Watson Tell Us about Potential Future Expert-Systems," *Silicon Angle*, February 2011.

12. Daniel H. Pink, *A Whole New Mind: Why Right-Brainers Will Rule the Future*. New York, NY: Penguin, 2005 (p. 42).

13. "Vantage Learning Launches MY Access!(R) College Edition to Improve Writing Skills for Incoming Freshman," *Red Orbit*, April 2008.

14. Daniel H. Pink, Drive: *The Surprising Truth about What Motivates Us*. New York, NY: Riverhead Books, 2009 (p. 125).

Chapter 10

Applications for Individualizing Instruction

The future is not a goal; it is an achievement.
—Robert Kennedy, U.S. Senator and brother
of President J. F. Kennedy

Today, as the world becomes more diverse and complex, additional learning applications will be required to meet an ever-growing array of student needs. With the advent of computers and electronic media, individualized learning can be expanded to a greater degree.

Individualized learning needs can range from English as a second language, to CTE instruction, to remedial applications, and to advanced independent study or project work. Many educators believe that individualizing learning is too difficult for teachers to accomplish in today's large and diverse classrooms, but whatever the learning needs may be, there can be educational technology applications to meet them.

TUTORING IS INDIVIDUALIZED LEARNING

Individualizing instruction doesn't have to be difficult because, in fact, many of the principles for individualizing instruction have been around for a long time—through one-on-one tutoring. It is simply a recognition that different students will benefit from different paces, instructional approaches, and supporting content. A guiding principle of learning is that it will occur best when it fits within an individual's own knowledge structures and when it is meaningful and purposeful.[1]

One-on-one human tutoring has long been considered as the best form of instruction. The word *tutor* comes from the Latin word *tutus*, which means protector. Tutor has the additional meanings of safeguarding, watching over, promoting growth, and mentoring. These definitions can be easily contrasted with the term *lecturer*, which is the most commonly understood definition of an instructor.

In the same way that human tutoring has always provided the means to address individual student needs, computers can now be used for private tutoring and for supplemental learning needs. These opportunities can be introduced at the high school level so that varied student needs can be targeted.

Self-direction of learning can also begin at this time and be encouraged for all learners. But the important point to consider is that not all applications will be a good fit for all learners. There must be an identification of the learner characteristics as well as the goals of each student.

LESS STRUCTURED VS. MORE STRUCTURED APPROACHES

A primary characteristic of computerized learning is that the applications vary from more structured approaches to less structured approaches. It has long been known that students who are high achievers learn best with activities that are *less structured,* while students who are low achievers learn best with activities that are *more structured*. The high-achieving students are the ones who benefit the most from independent study or project work, while it is the lowest achievers who benefit the most from structured tutoring.

High achievement usually consists of two things. It is having the prior knowledge in a subject area, but it is also very much meta-cognitive ability and good study skills. Since meta-cognitive ability generally grows with academic achievement, students who have had the most academic success (high achievers) usually can handle the most complex and ill-structured activities. On the other hand, students who do not have sufficient background knowledge and meta-cognitive skills (low achievers) will require applications that both are supportive of their lack of background knowledge and well structured so as to guide them through the learning process.

Ironically, it is the less structured methods which are oftentimes not preferred by high-achieving students because the goals are less clear, and the students think they have less of a chance for an "A" grade. High-achieving students may say they prefer learning in a structured environment, but it is really because of the perceived easy success. They actually learn more and will become more intrinsically motivated from less structured or independent methods.

Consequently, low achievers may indicate that they would enjoy a low-structure, low-profile task such as independent project work, but it is these hard-to-teach students that need the most direction with supportive feedback that is found in most structured computerized applications. They will feel the motivation and intrinsic rewards after they have been successful with the task.

All students should be challenged with content and activities in which they have no choice but to cope and respond. Their capabilities will grow and even surprise them. The important point is that certain applications will be a better fit for some students as opposed to others, and there needs to be a variety of methods to use. There are many technology applications that can be used to individualize instruction including *empowering environments, Internet learning, distance learning, and computer-assisted instruction (CAI)*.

EMPOWERING ENVIRONMENTS

Empowering environments are software programs that can perform the routine or time-consuming parts of a task that frees up the student for more creative thinking and expression. There are empowering environments in a large variety of subject areas including art, writing, and speaking.

Take, for example, the field of art. The goal of artistic creation is really to transfer mental images to a medium such as a canvas so that others can share in the artist's experiences and emotions. However, rather than sharing their ideas and experiences, most people usually have to spend large amounts of time mixing colors as well as learning the mechanisms of using the brush correctly. They have to be very precise when they are painting, and they cannot make any mistakes.

Now, when using graphics arts programs, people can be exposed to an unlimited palette of colors, styles, and brush strokes from which to choose. They can alter, pixel by pixel, the contour of an image, and they can instantly "undo" any mistakes. Artists can be involved with the creative aspects of painting while the empowering environment handles the mechanics. As noted by one teacher,

> I rediscovered my love of art using Photoshop, drawing tools in Microsoft Office, Flash, and recently, the myriad of apps for my iOS and Android devices—to awaken the frustrated artist in you. "Creative confidence is like a muscle—it can be strengthened and nurtured through effort and experience."[2]

Consequently, computerized word processing programs have transformed the area of writing and composition. Standard word processing programs have allowed writers to spend more time revising and polishing their work.

Evidence strongly supports the fact that students are writing more when they use word processing software.[3] Having the ability to frequently correct errors and revise written content has made the entire writing process more flexible and creative.

Speaking skills are also being enhanced through presentation software like PowerPoint. Presentation software has shown an amazing ability to motivate learners to do complex presentations. Using computer software programs for word processing, oral presentations, and graphic arts productions must be practiced in order to improve on them.

> The most difficult thing for students seems to be creating order out of chaos. They often get overwhelmed by a project's detail and options because they did not start with a message, purpose, and audience. Technology can help students create a skeleton structure to map thoughts by using styles in word processing and outline view in slide shows.[4]

These applications can finally help students to "get something done," because they can provide scaffolding and tools to get started. It is important for students to learn *all* the steps for successful project creation. Using multimedia applications can greatly enhance this process, by allowing students to utilize the features of the application to help in the project's creation.

The very important area of *media literacy* can be further enhanced when students use multiple mediums of text, graphics, audio, automation, and digital images within presentations.

> As with other constructivist learning strategies, students will learn more deeply when constructing meaning through demonstrated understanding. The use of multimedia dramatically enhances student learning.[5]

Students will learn more fully by repeatedly completing more projects in varying levels of difficulty. The scope and difficulty of the project can be varied for each student. When added to a digital portfolio, student work can speak for itself without the need for ranking and grading.

INTERNET LEARNING

When students gain information from the Internet, they can search for the best solution path or intellectual "quest." The Internet really provides a learning environment that is consistent with how Darwinian evolutionary theory states the optimal learning environment should be. Namely, that the potential for intelligence to grow is in proportion to the diversity in the environment.[6] The Internet provides that diversity.

In today's busy world, the time that people have to gain knowledge is limited. However, the amount of information available for reference is becoming greater and greater. For this reason, the ability to quickly and accurately find information from the Internet will comprise most knowledge-gathering requirements.

Activities using the Internet can range from retrieving simple facts to performing complex data analysis. Locating information and reporting on it is a very basic activity that can be done by mostly anyone, while more advanced learners can do such challenging tasks as finding information for critical data analysis. As learners grow in their research capabilities, they can be successful at more difficult tasks.

Research work in the future will consist of more than gathering information, but instead will comprise of the precise interpretation and organization of it as well. For example, as noted in one book in relation to investigating global warming:

> In laying out the typical questions and data useful to investigate the potential impact of global warming, a general framework is used in which students specialize by selecting a country, its specific data, and the particular issue for the project focus (e.g., rise in carbon dioxide emissions due to recent growth, deforestation, floods due to rising sea levels). Students then investigate either a global issue or the point of view of a single country and consider current results of international policy in light of their project findings.[7]

It is important for older students to have opportunities to work independently or in groups using the Internet to investigate real-world issues. Their skills in research analysis can improve from simple to complex, and they can be deeply engaged in the process as well. However, it is important that the level of the learning is matched to the ability level and interest of the students.

Visual literacy can also be greatly enhanced through Web-based learning. While pictures have always been a complement to written text, they are now advancing to a higher level through the Internet.

> The subject of visual learning was explored first through the gathering of images. Editing and drawing tools were introduced and images from lessons were edited and inserted into drawings. The next installment of visual learning content involved presentation, featuring a slide show project as well as a quick lesson on creating and editing sound files. This set the stage for animation and video editing.[8]

Since content is increasingly being presented through video and images, it is important for students to begin to research and communicate in this way. This can also assist those students for whom English is a second language.

Gathering pictures and images on the Internet can help lower achievers receive more confidence in the data-gathering process.

Internet learning can further promote self-directed learning. Since the desire to direct one's learning becomes more pronounced as people grow older, there should be opportunities for students to self-direct some of their learning—select topics of their choice. With appropriate practice, anyone, including low achievers, can learn how to become lifelong learners.

Project-based learning through the Internet can be the way to help learners acquire the skills to become lifelong learners. Once learners are in control of their own learning, it becomes enjoyable. They will understand and feel the rewards.

DISTANCE LEARNING

The distance learning movement began as a way for busy adults to attend courses when they didn't live near a college or university. It has expanded to a much larger range of applications to bring more learning to more people. It is currently being used to extend the course offerings of many schools. Students can take foreign language courses, AP courses, or other courses not available in their school setting.

However, students need to have good meta-cognitive abilities and study skills to be successful in these courses. They must pace and monitor their own progress, and oftentimes wait extended periods of time for feedback on activities and tests. Unfortunately, these courses continue to have a stubbornly high dropout rate. In this regard, distance learning is a much less-structured activity than normal classroom instruction, and consequently works best with *high-achieving* students. As one book on distance learning concludes:

> A successful online student has the desire to learn and is willing to make the sacrifices of time and effort to do so. Maturity seems to be linked to motivation. Students who enrolled in distance education tended to be older and more serious and to share such characteristics as self-discipline, higher expectations and motivation.[9]

The promise of distance learning can be compared to another previous educational enhancement—the correspondence course. After national mail service was instituted, many people believed there would be a revolution in education because now any person, even in the most remote locations, could take courses and become educated. However, it did not work out that way because only a small percentage of strongly motivated people actually chose to take correspondence courses and were successful with them.

Since distance learning courses can work for those students who can handle its independent nature, these courses can be used for supplemental and independent learning at the high school level and beyond. Students can take college-level courses or other advanced course work as associated with their goals for the future. They can also take specialized courses with other students who share their achievement abilities and interest and then do related group project work together, which can be highly motivating. As one statement by an article on university business schools indicated:

> Business schools have their uses but they overstate what they can deliver and may be unintentionally letting down their products—the students—by forgoing real-world learning for the classroom. The growing popularity of part-time executive programs is one response to this criticism—a reliance on distance learning, with lectures delivered over the internet, supplemented with tutorial groups in the student's own locality. The students are encouraged to relate every set of concepts to their situation in essays, thus cementing the learning in their own experience.[10]

Distance learning can link students with professionals in all parts of the country and the world. This benefit will become increasingly important as the world of work becomes more technical and specialized. Communication and future learning can happen after the course is completed as students stay connected through emails, social media practices, or even internships.

Within CTE learning, students can take distance learning courses provided by trade schools or other private sector schools in preparation for their goals for the future. This can often be motivating enough for the student to want to continue to learn in the area, providing an important "foot-in-the-door" to postsecondary education.

COMPUTER-ASSISTED INSTRUCTION (CAI)

Computer-assisted instruction (CAI) is instruction delivered solely through the computer. The most common type of CAI is the *tutorial*. Each tutorial module has the benefit of structured content, practice, and feedback programmed in. Another important benefit is that students can proceed at their own pace. Through testing or choice processes, these programs can align instruction to the precise ability level of the learners.[11]

CAI is a highly structured learning activity, so it is most beneficial for *low-achieving students,* and, in some instances, has been a major factor in reducing the dropout rate. Within a classic Florida high school program study, dramatic results were achieved with computer-assisted instruction. Students who had failed throughout their school years were, for the first time, experiencing academic success. These were young people who felt helpless and alienated in the classroom.

> Previously, a (Florida high) school had been having difficulty in retaining 60% of at-risk students. With computer instruction, their retention rate skyrocketed, eventually to over 80%. Moreover, an unexpected revelation jolted pupils; school could be fun.[12]

Tutorials can be an important supplement to traditional academic subjects to help bring lower-achieving students up to proficiency. Many tutorials, such as *Khan Academy*, are free and available to assist learners in a virtually unlimited range of academic content.

In addition to assisting lower-achieving students with traditional academic coursework, tutorials can be utilized by higher achieving students as well. As the world becomes more complex and diverse, CAI will increasingly be a learning tool of choice when it used for individual student needs. In most cases, when people are interested in learning an entirely new subject, they will view a video tutorial on the subject.

When learners complete very specific learning that they need at one particular time, it is often referred to as "just-in-time." Just-in-time learning is an adult learning method often utilized within business and industry. And, evidence strongly supports the fact that when instruction is "just-in-time" for older learners, attention, motivation, and retention tend to be higher.[13]

Older students should have opportunities to take "just-in-time" learning according to their needs, interests, and goals. They will increasingly need this skill in the future. Students can take a tutorial, for example, to learn knowledge in order to complete a project. These skills will be greatly needed in the workplace and should be introduced before students enter the workforce.

Whether it is for completely self-paced, remedial instruction, or just-in-time learning, tutorials can play a valuable role in supplementing learning, especially at the high school level and beyond.

BLENDED LEARNING

Blended learning is a combination of classroom and computerized instruction. Individualized learning alongside traditional classroom instruction can assist both slow and fast learners to achieve the kind of success that is often not possible in today's "one-size-fits-all" classroom. Once students are comfortable with an individualized approach, they can begin to achieve on their own like experts have done throughout time. As noted in one book:

> Blended learning has the potential to revolutionize K–12 education in terms of quality and cost because it allows for a more consistent and personalized pedagogy, requires fewer specialized teachers, and uses space efficiently.[14]

In addition to improving academic and real-world skills, students also need choices in the activities and projects they complete. As students grow older, they become increasingly aware that certain activities are more personally enjoyable than others. Students may discover they enjoy playing a musical instrument or reading science fiction. Of course, on top of most every teenager's category of interests are popular technologies like video games. These devices are extremely instructionally rewarding because they provide continuous feedback and they allow for mastery.

Many people have advocated putting strict restriction on student's outside activities of interests like video games, so they will not interfere with schoolwork. Whatever negative characteristics can be attributed to these out-of-school activities, the unfortunate truth is that many students are finding them more personally rewarding than much of what they are learning in school. And as most parents know, if restrictions are imposed on these undesirable activities, then they are going to be facing a very rebellious teenager.

Instead of enforcing restrictions on undesirable activities of student interest like video games, make the video games part of the instruction plan. Student are likely to be most appreciative that enjoyable activities are becoming part of the educational process.

MORE INDIVIDUALIZED LEARNING IN THE FUTURE

Whether it is learning basic skills or complex concepts, there will increasingly be learning needs that will challenge any teacher. Teachers must begin to consider individual student achievement instead of only group achievement, but they are facing a larger and more diverse group of students and are responsible for the achievement of all of their students. This can require extraordinary efforts. Some students seem "un-teachable." To many, it can often feel it is too difficult to meet each student's needs while still meeting the needs of all the other students.

Like any field, teachers start out with knowing only the basic ways to teach. In time, teachers develop professional competencies and a virtual database of ideas for imparting knowledge. They understand that there are many different ways to learn. Structured instruction with guidance and feedback may be appropriate for some students. Others will excel when presented with open-ended questions and problems to consider.

In addition, the purpose for learning is also expanding. It is no longer just for enlightenment, but also for imparting specific knowledge and skills required for a student's success in the future. Schools are required to teach basic knowledge and skills but also required to teach what is required for work and life.

Teachers must come to know their students as individuals. What are their needs? What are their goals? These needs and goals must be met by a variety of ways, and there must be prescriptions for solutions. It is important for educators to react proactively to these challenges and show results. The time is now.

CHAPTER 10—KEY POINTS TO REMEMBER

- Empowering environments let technology handle the difficult aspects of a task, freeing up the mind for greater learning. They are highly motivating and can promote real-world skill development.
- Internet learning is a powerful way and individualized self expression for students to proceed according to their own intellectual quest. Internet learning can be varied from simple to complex depending on the student group.
- Distance learning can provide courses to students not available at the student's location. However, it is the nonstructured activity that works best with high-achieving students. CTE courses can also be successful with students who are highly motivated to learn in those areas.
- CAI is a highly structured activity that allows for students to proceed at their own pace. It works best with lower-achieving students but has the capability to be expanded to more uses when used for "just-in-time" learning.

NOTES

1. S. Brookfield, "Self-Directed Learning: A Critical Review of Research," In S. Brookfield (Ed.), *Self-Directed Learning: From Theory to Practice,* 1985 (pp. 17–30).

2. Sharon "SAM" Sakai-Miller, *Innovation Age Learning—Empowering Students by Empowering Teachers*. Arlington, VA: ISTE, 2016, (p. 102).

3. Stewart Brand, *The Media Lab: Inventing the Future at MIT*. New York, NY: Viking Penguin Inc., 1987 (p. 253).

4. Sharon "SAM" Sakai-Miller, *Innovation Age Learning – Empowering Students by Empowering Teachers*. Arlington, VA: ISTE, 2016, (p. 69).

5. Sharon "SAM" Sakai-Miller, *Innovation Age Learning—Empowering Students by Empowering Teachers*. Arlington, VA: ISTE, 2016 (p. 76).

6. G. Marchioni, "Hypermedia and Learning: Freedom and Chaos," *Educational Technology*, 28(1), 1988, (pp. 8–11).

7. National Academy of Sciences, *How People Learn: Brain, Mind Experience, and School*, Washington, DC: National Academy Press, 2000 (p. 213).

8. Sharon "SAM" Sakai-Miller, *Innovation Age Learning—Empowering Students by Empowering Teachers*. Arlington, VA: ISTE, 2016 (p. 38).

9. Gene I. Maeroff, *A Classroom of One: How Online Learning Is Changing Our Schools and Colleges*, New York, NY: Palgrave Macmillan, 2003 (p. 105).

10. Charles Handy, "You Can't Learn Management in a Classroom," *USA Today*, January 28, 2008.

11. William Horton, *Designing Web-Based Training*, New York, NY: Wiley, 2000 (pp. 136–148).

12. B. Gross, "Can Computer-Assisted Instruction Solve the Dropout Problem?" *Educational Leadership*, 46(5), 1989 (pp. 49–51).

13. Allen Collins and Richard Halverson, *Rethinking Education in the Age of Technology; The Digital Revolution and Schooling in America*. New York, NY: Teachers College Press, 2009 (p. 27).

14. Sharon "SAM" Sakai-Miller, *Innovation Age Learning—Empowering Students by Empowering Teachers*. Arlington, VA: ISTE, 2016, (p. 57).

Chapter 11

Conclusion

Genius is 1% inspiration and 99% perspiration.
—Thomas Alva Edison

There are clearly many ways to incorporate technology into learning, but practical reasons alone can prevent this. Education lacks methods to research and test new ideas. There is no way to know how to successfully implement new initiatives. Within business and industry, it is only improvements with clear measurable results which are continued. There is a considered return on investment (ROI) on any chosen approach. A similar focus of return on investment also needs to be emphasized with educational technology integration, as stated below.

> [For] successful reform initiatives: (1) They improve the quality in school for teachers and for students by making school a more exciting, involving place to be, (2) They seem to make many kinds of learning more effective and efficient and thus raise students achievements in a wide diverse assortment of classrooms, (3) They thrive and grow, moving from school to school and state to state because educators and students—not just regulators or academic theorists—champion them, (4) They make it possible for teachers to handle larger classes without sacrificing their effectiveness.[1]

Improving quality for both teachers and students will require a shared approach to redesign. To make learning more effective and efficient in varied educational settings with varied learners requires an "all of the above approach." Instead of finding the one best method to work in all cases, many applications should be utilized in varied settings along with a sharing of results and effects.

In the case of the ideas expressed in this book, one conceptual framework that could be utilized to implement technology is according to the three memory types in the brain: *semantic, episodic, and procedural* memories. Since each of these three areas can contain a large number of applications, educators could begin to incorporate apps from each category. There could be a sharing of results and best practices. But there could also be choice within the three areas so that the applications could best fit the characteristics and needs of each student group.

For example, a higher-achieving school district would likely choose more academically advanced applications than a lower-achieving school district. There should be choices for educators to find the best fit.

IMPROVING KNOWLEDGE-BASED LEARNING

In the case of knowledge-based (semantic) learning there are two primary ways that technology could be implemented in this area. The first, of course, is to increase achievement in general academic learning. Students proceed at different learning paces. Some progress quickly through academic material, while some require additional time and instruction. Tutorials can be provided to those who fall behind.

Tutorials are highly structured, self-paced and provide needed guidance and feedback. A common problem today is that students often enter college unprepared. They must take remedial courses before they can take courses in their chosen field or major, and they are often required to pay for these remedial courses as well. If students' academic skills are below what is required, they should take tutorials *before* they go to college.

An easy way to consider how this process could be implemented is by considering how learning occurs for students who have dropped out of high school. I had the opportunity to visit and converse with a class of students preparing to take the HiSET, high school equivalency test. Students in the HiSET prep courses do tutorial work on a computer alongside instructors who monitor their progress and assist with pinpointing their needs and goals. Once students are able to pass the HiSET test, they are considered ready for community college. High schools need to ensure that students are academically ready for, at minimum, community college. As stated in the immensely compelling book *The Case against Education*:

> Here's the real crisis: every year, over a million students who won't graduate start college. Their failure is foreseeable; high school students with poor grades and low-test scores rarely earn BAs. Instead of tempting marginal students with cheap credit, we should bluntly warn them that college is stacked against them.[2]

This same process used in high school equivalency programs could be implemented within high schools. If every student took the HiSET test, there could be an accurate gauging of who has achieved the basic skills needed for college, and who requires additional instruction. The last two years of high school could be devoted to ensuring that the basic reading, writing, and math skills have been achieved.

Technology can also greatly assist those who are progressing at a fast pace academically. For those students who have achieved what is required on the HiSET, and beyond, whole distance learning courses can be provided in the final years of high school. For those students who are proceeding at a rapid pace, they can work together on advanced online courses. When like-minded students work together, there will be shared motivation and interest. It is an easy and inexpensive way to increase achievement for those students who are high-achieving and gifted.

But in addition to improving standard achievement, a second way to improve knowledge-based (semantic) learning is to promote better and deeper concept learning. It means providing more cases to allow students to receive a better understanding. Let them play a game? Let them explore an issue through a project that utilizes an empowering environment.

> Give students numerous and diverse options. Instead of making students study yet another American poem, expose them to Japanese graphic novels. Rather than forcing kids to perform one more play, show them a few films from the 1980s. If you want to help kids discover what emotionally "clicks" for them, use trial and error.[3]

Most school learning is heavy on concept learning, so the concept learning could benefit from more cases. Today's students are often not learning concepts deeply enough to be able to truly understand and manipulate the knowledge in meaningful ways. They should have opportunities to choose the methods that are most engaging for them.

Students are now required to absorb larger and more complex amounts of information, but they are required to do much more than that. They will need to find ways to sort through and utilize the vast amounts of knowledge available in our digitized world in beneficial ways. This requires them to process, manipulate, and create from the knowledge they absorb.

It means going beyond simple comprehension to analysis and synthesis of the knowledge as well. If educators made it a priority to assign a certain number of technology applications to augment learning, many can be chosen and applied, and it would move the process forward of determining what works best in each situation.

IMPROVING EXPERIENTIAL-BASED LEARNING

Using technology to improve experiential (episodic) learning will greatly increase interest and motivation in students. By introducing students to real-world events, they will be able to directly experience the learning and they will *want* to learn more. It is simply the recognition that school needs to become more interesting to students. A way to do this is to add experiential learning.

> Why so bored (in high school)? Eighty-two percent say the material isn't interesting, 41% say the material isn't relevant. No wonder a major Gates foundation study ranked boredom as the MOST important reason why kids drop out of high school.[4]

There need to be applications for which the sole purpose is to create interest and excitement in the students. For example, in the book and movie *The Freedom Writer's Diary*, "Ms. G." is charged with instructing students from very poor social and economic situations. Many of these teens are actively involved with gangs. In her desperation to reach them, she inadvertently mentions the Holocaust, which mildly grabs their attention. After Ms. G. realizes this interest, she begins to focus her curriculum around the events of the Holocaust.

She first takes her students to the Holocaust Museum so they can better experience those events. Since many of her students had been victims of violence themselves within their neighborhoods, visiting the museum was a very meaningful experience to them. They were able to relate and "feel" the negative aspects of the Holocaust. After her students had visited the Holocaust Museum, Ms. G. assigns them the book *The Diary of Anne Frank* to read. For many students in her class, this was the first book they actually read with meaning and understanding in their lives.[5] When media and experiential-based learning events are available in a large variety of topics, teachers can better match the needs and interests of their students without having to expend extraordinary time and resources.

> If you want school to work, don't bribe or threaten people. Show them what it's like to succeed. Give them a taste of the work required and let them play with it. If kids need to learn about predators and prey, among a million other things, let them be the predators and prey. Let them make mistakes and help one another. Eventually they'll figure it out for themselves and take pleasure in it.[6]

There are many applications available now, such as virtual museums, that can be used by teachers to make education more meaningful and engaging.

Chapter 11

IMPROVING SKILL-BASED LEARNING

In the same way that knowledge-based learning can be improved in two ways, skill-based learning can also be improved in two ways. In regard to general academic skills, drill-and-practice and academic simulations can improve in this area. Skills rely on practice, so practice needs to be increased, especially as academic content becomes more difficult. It isn't only the lower-achieving students who can benefit from additional drill-and-practice programs, every student can benefit from "overlearning" basic skills and that comes from additional practice.

In addition to improving general academic skills, students should have opportunities to have additional practice in advanced areas where they have interest. It can take up to ten years to become an expert, and students can hone into their areas of interest while still in high school. With additional practice that they provide for themselves, they can achieve a certain level in a game or simulation, create an algorithm to solve a problem, or determine a hypothesis to solve a problem in the real world.

> In the words of K. Anders Ericsson, the world's leading expert on expertise, novices improve as long as they are (1) given a task with a well-defined goal, (2) motivated to improve, (3) provided with feedback, and (4) provided with ample opportunities for repetition and gradual refinements of their performance.[7]

Students can also benefit highly from more practice of general technology skills. This is an area that is solely lacking in education today, but students can practice improving their technology skills in all areas. It had generally been a concern among educators about the teaching of technology skills because of the training and expertise required by teachers in order to instruct in this area. But this doesn't need to be the case. Students can learn these apps on their own. They can view instructional videos on sites such as YouTube or take microlearning apps on the Internet. They can learn the technology skills first, and then complete a project with it.

> Because technology tools are ubiquitous in all disciplines of study and careers, deliberate pairings would ensure that students have broad exposure to and proficiency with technology tools. In other words, if teachers take the same careful approach toward accruing technology skills [as academic skills], students will develop their technology-infused projects more efficiently.[8]

Having performance-based grading that is listed separately on a grading sheet is one way for students to master technology skills. Once again, there is no A, B, C, D, F for learning most real-world skills, but only a criterion level of achievement. It means receiving certifications for acquired skills.

Apprenticeships and internships are also a way to learn real-world skills by actually performing them. Many countries in Europe have had a long commitment to apprenticeship programs. In the last years of high school, internships and apprenticeships could be included through an individualized plan. Schools can make arrangements with local employers to have students work at an employer site for a portion of the school day and to get credit for this.

Apprenticeship programs can provide a better and more successful future for many students, especially those who do not want to attend a traditional university. But even within European apprenticeship programs, there is an understanding that today's apprenticeships must contain a higher level of knowledge than in the past. In Germany, this increasing emphasis on academic knowledge and skill development is referred to as the *dual system*. Within the United States, students wanting to complete an apprenticeship or internship can take related coursework through distance learning or community college courses.

PROMOTING SELF-DIRECTED AND LIFELONG LEARNING

Currently, students are self-directing their learning through computer games, social media, and the Internet. They should begin to be able to self-direct their learning within formal education. High school is a perfect time to launch students into self-directed learning where they can begin to develop the metacognitive skills and motivation to become lifelong learners. Increasing their skill level is something they will have to face throughout their lives. They may need some guidance in their pursuits, but all students can acquire the capabilities to become lifelong learners.

It seems to be the first law of human nature that if you want to improve a process, then you should directly involve those persons who are most impacted by that process. W. Edwards Deming would certainly agree with that. Deming revolutionized the world of manufacturing by allowing those persons who were doing the manufacturing labor to be the ones who determined how best to improve the manufacturing process. It is the *students* who are most impacted by their learning, yet their role in the learning process has always been limited. Students will most likely achieve at a higher level in those areas that they find most interesting and relevant to their lives.

Most older learners will possess one or more readiness limitations. These may include poverty, a dysfunctional home life, or racial/cultural barriers. It can signal to the learner that they are not "up to par" with others. This is where the benefits of computers and technology can really be utilized to account for a variety of backgrounds, academic strengths and weaknesses. In a country as large and diverse as the United States, students must have ways to "rise above" their varied limitations and use their natural strengths and abilities to guide them.

Most importantly for the future of education is to promote the metacognitive and motivational skills required for students to be lifelong learners. Many people are uncomfortable with machines teaching. One person teaching another person is one of the most fundamentally human interactions that we know. But a computer operates according to the programming commands that a human prescribed. In this regard, it is only a reflection of a human's teaching ability. It is an enhancement like any other technique to increase the potential for learning.

How can learning success be assured in both academic and nonacademic settings, and especially in the long run? The answer most certainly lies in individualized and real-world adaptive learning. It is the realization of a student's potential that will have the greatest impact on achievement. It is the power that resides within.

NOTES

1. Kenneth G. Wilson, *Redesigning Education—A Nobel Prize Winner Reveals What Must Be Done to Reform American Education*. New York: Teachers College Press, Columbia University, 1994 (p. 157).

2. Bryan Caplan, *The Case against Education—Why the Education System Is a Waste of Time and Money*. Princeton, NJ: Princeton University Press, 2016 (p. 277).

3. Bryan Caplan, *The Case against Education—Why the Education System Is a Waste of Time and Money*. Princeton, NJ: Princeton University Press, 2016 (p. 256).

4. Bryan Caplan, *The Case against Education—Why the Education System Is a Waste of Time and Money*. Princeton, NJ: Princeton University Press, 2016 (p. 256).

5. Erin Gruwell and the Freedom Writers, *The Freedom Writers Diary: How a Teacher and 150 Teens Used Writing to Change Themselves and the World around Them*, New York, NY: Broadway Books, 2009.

6. Greg Toppo, *The Game Believes in You—How Digital Play Can Make Our Kids Smarter*. New York: Palgrave Macmillan, 2015 (p. 139).

7. Bryan Caplan, *The Case Against Education—Why the Education System Is a Waste of Time and Money*, New Jersey: Princeton University Press, 2016 (p. 63).

8. Sharon "SAM" Salai-Miller, *Innovation Age Learning—Empowering Students by Empowering Teachers*. Arlington, VA: ISTE, 2016 (p. 28).

Index

Academic skill development, 3–4, 56–68, 88–96, 111, 114
Adult learning, 3, 4, 61–62, 96
Affective domain, learning in, 37–38, 113
Albert Bandura, theories of, 35–36
Algorithms, 54
Andragogy, 3, 4, 61–62
Aptitudes in learning, 16–17, 37–38
Artificial intelligence (AI), 94–96
Automaticity, 13, 43, 58, 88–89, 114

Behaviorism, 41–42
Benjamin Bloom, theories of, 13, 16
Blended learning, 106–107
Brainstorming, 55
Buggy models, 93–94

Caste system, 3
Cattell, James M., theories of, 15–16
Charles Spearmen, theories of, 14
Children's style of learning, 6, 9–10, 48–49, 77, 96
Chunking, 69–70
Cognitive skill learning, 13–14, 43, 56–59, 88–91, 114
Computational bias, 11–2, 56–7
Computer-assisted instruction (CAI), 105–106

Context, 22, 82–83
Control in learning, 2, 6, 49, 70–75
Creating a knowledge base, 34–35
CTE learning, 37, 43, 58–59, 89–91, 114
Cultural background, 24–25, 47–48

Deliberate practice, 68
Dewey, John, theories of, 52
Discovery learning, 92–93
Distance learning, 104–105
Distinctiveness, 78
Drill and practice, 43, 69–70, 88–89, 114

Education reform, 1–2, 110
Empowering environments, 101–102
Episodic memory, 11–12, 30–32
Experiential learning, 5–6, 11–12, 36–38, 56–57, 113

Feedback, 42, 56, 73
Flow states, 60
Forgetting, preventing, 81–82; in context to prevent, 82–83
Formal operational stage, 10

Games in learning, 5–6, 22, 91–93
G-factor of intelligence, 14–15

Grit factor, 96
Group learning, 60–61, 104

Howard Gardner, theories of, 16, 56–57

Insightful learning, 55–56, 92
Instructional Design Model, 44
Intelligence, 14–17
Internet learning, 102–105

Jerome Bruner, theories of, 92–93

Knowledge, 20–22; organization of, 22–23; improvement of, 111–112; base of, 34–35
Knowles, Malcolm, 3–4, 61–62

Learner characteristics, 23–24, 100–101
Lifelong learning, 4, 70–75, 100
Long-term memory, 68–69

Maslow, Abraham, theories of, 48
Meaningfulness, 65–66, 70–75, 78–79, 99–100
Media literacy, 32–33, 102–103,
Media, to enhance learning, 32–34, 78, 56–59, 89–91, 113
Memorization, rote, 67–68; improving, 77–79, 82; chunking to improve, 69–70; spacing to improve, 68
Meta-cognition, 2, 6, 49, 70–75
Megatrends references, 1, 2, 4, 58
Mnemonics and stories to improve memory, 80–81
Modeling, 35–36
Motivation, 2, 3, 37–38, 49, 70–17

Openness of U.S. education, 3

Participatory culture, 36–37, 101–102, 113
Pedagogy, 3, 4, 61, 82
Performance based testing, 84–85

Piaget, Jean, theories of, 9–10, 30
Portfolio work, 49, 84
Practice, 12, 43–44, 56–59, 88–96, 111, 114
Procedural memory, 12–14, 41–42, 52–53
Programmed Instruction, 41–43, 69–70, 105
Purposeful learning, 65–66, 72–75, 78, 99–100

Rate in learning, 25, 43, 99–100
Readiness to learn, 24, 69–70
Real-world skill development, 3–4, 43–44, 58–59, 88–93, 101–102, 114
Reasoning, deductive, 52, 54; inductive, 54–55; reflective, 56–57, 92–93
Rehearsal, 67–68
Rewards in learning, extrinsic, 45; intrinsic, 45–46, 73–74

Scientific method, 54–55
Self-directed learning, 4, 72–75, 115
Semantic memory, 9–10, 20–22
Senses, learning through, 11–12, 30–32, 113
Sesame Street, 33–34
Short-term memory, 67–68
Simulations, 13–14, 43–44, 56–69, 89–91
Skills, 12–14, 35–36, 56; Academic, 43, 50–57; 114 Real-world, 43–44, 58, 114–115
Skinner, B.F., theories of, 41–42, 46–47
Spacing effect, 68
Standardized learning, 3, 5, 26–28
Sternberg, Robert, theories of, 17–18
Structured vs. less structured learning, 23–24, 41–43, 100–105
Study skills, 71–72
Style in learning, 25, 26

Task-based learning, 84–86
Teacher and student relationship, 1, 42, 115
Testing, 83–84; performance-based, 84–85
Tulving, Endel, theories of, 9
Tutorials, 43, 69–70, 111

Underachievement, 43, 69–70, 70–75, 100–101, 105–106

Virtual reality, 35, 78, 113
Visuals, learning through, 30–32, 78, 56–59, 89–91, 113

About the Authors

Christine Bernat is a technical writer and instructional designer who has worked for many information technology companies. She has a bachelor's degree in psychology and a master's degree in education (instructional technology). She has a strong background and interest in adult learning and instructional design principles. Visit her website at www.learnthroughlife.com.

Richard J. Mueller's career encompassed thirty years as a professor of educational psychology, and he has written four textbooks and numerous articles. Mueller had a master's degree and a PhD in educational psychology. Prior to receiving his advanced degrees, Mueller worked as a junior high school and high school English and social studies teacher. Mueller passed away in 2005.

www.ingramcontent.com/pod-product-compliance
Lightning Source LLC
Chambersburg PA
CBHW051814230426
43672CB00012B/2737